The GOD of the MOUNTAIN

BOOK III

Wherefore HE SAITH, When He ascended up on high, he led captivity captive, AND GAVE GIFTS UNTO MEN. ...

And HE GAVE SOME, Apostles; and some, Prophets; and some, Evangelists; and some, Pastors and Teachers;
For the perfecting of the saints,
for the work of the ministry,
for the edifying of the Body of Christ:
Till WE ALL COME IN THE UNITY OF THE FAITH, and of the knowledge of the Son of God, unto a perfect man, unto the measure of the stature of the fulness of Christ:

Ephesians 4:8, 11-13 KJV

The GOD of the MOUNTAIN

BOOK III

Written by various Authors
(See Contents for a complete list of Authors)

A BOLD TRUTH Publication
Christian Literature & Artwork

The GOD of the MOUNTAIN (BOOK III)
Copyright © 2020 Aaron D. Jones
ISBN 13: 978-1-949993-28-8

First Edition

BOLD TRUTH PUBLISHING
(Christian Literature & Artwork)
606 West 41st, Ste. 4
Sand Springs, Oklahoma 74063
www.BoldTruthPublishing.com

Available from Amazon.com and other retail outlets. Orders by U.S. trade bookstores and wholesalers. Email: *boldtruthbooks@yahoo.com*

Quantity sales special discounts are available on quantity purchases by corporations, associations, and others. For details, contact the publisher at the address above.

Artwork, formatting and overall design by Aaron Jones.

All rights reserved under International Copyright Law. All contents and/or cover art and design may not be reproduced in whole or in part in any form without the express written consent of the Author.

Printed in the USA.
05 20   10 9 8 7 6 5 4 3 2 1

Permissions

Scripture quotations marked "AMP" are taken from the Amplified® Bible, Copyright © 1954, 1958, 1962, 1964, 1965, 1987 by The Lockman Foundation. Used by permission.

"Scripture quotations taken from the Amplified® Bible *Classic Edition* (AMPC), Copyright © 1954, 1958, 1962, 1964, 1965, 1987 by The Lockman Foundation. Used by permission. www.Lockman.org"

Many of the unmarked Scripture quotations and those marked KJV are taken from the King James Version of The Bible. [Public Domain]

Scriptures marked NKJV are taken from the NEW KING JAMES VERSION (NKJV): Scripture taken from the NEW KING JAMES VERSION®. Copyright© 1982 by Thomas Nelson, Inc. Used by permission. All rights reserved.

"Scripture quotations marked NIV are taken from the Holy Bible, New International Version®. NIV®. Copyright © 1973, 1978, 1984 by International Bible Society. Used by permission of Zondervan. All rights reserved."

"Scripture quotations marked (NLT) are taken from the Holy Bible, New Living Translation, Copyright © 1996, 2004, 2007 by Tyndale House Foundation. Used by permission of Tyndale House Publishers, Inc., Carol Stream, IL 60188. All rights reserved."

Scripture quotations marked TPT are from The Passion

Permissions

Translation®. Copyright © 2017, 2018 by Passion & Fire Ministries, Inc. Used by permission. All rights reserved. ThePassionTranslation.com.

Contents by Author

FOREWORD *by Adrienne Gottlieb* i

ACKNOWLEDGMENTS iii

INTRODUCTION v

- *Allen, Rachel*
THE STORY OF LITTLE JAKEY 64

- *Andrews, Jim*
A BRAND NEW HEART 52
DOG WITH KIDNEY FAILURE—HEALED 100
THE DEAD CAME BACK TO LIFE 158

- *Andrews, Sharon*
SINGLE & TRUSTING GOD FOR A MATE 17

- *Batty, Jeane*
THE GIFT OF THE ANOINTING 47

- *Beattie, Darla Faye*
FROM EMPTINESS TO A FLAME 58

- *Bridges, Ginny*
GOD IS ON YOUR SIDE 5
SOLD OUT TO GOD'S MISSION 68
STEREOTYPES 86
DO YOU WANT A VISITATION 91
TESTIMONY TO INSPIRE 104
THE DNA OF GOD IN US 128
HE'S ALWAYS WITH US 140
FOCUSED ON THE PRIZE 150

- *Brophy, Renée Dowling*
GOD IS GOOD 71

Contents

- *Burnes, Marcella O'Banion*
LOVE LIFTED ME 33
A PRAYER OF THANKSGIVING 89
THIS IS WHAT YOU ARE 120
THE HARVEST IS RIPE
BATTLE STATIONS, BATTLE CALL 156
LIFE AND DEATH; DEATH AND LIFE
BIRTHING PAINS 172

- *Clancy, Marty*
AN AMAZING MIRACLE 28
MAINTAINING A TEACHABLE SPIRIT ...93
POWER OF GOD VS.
INTELLECTUAL CHRISTIANITY 139
HEAVEN KNOWS DAD 178

- *Conley, Steven*
AWE 106

- *Farmer, Steve*
GOD KEEPS CONFIRMING HIS WORD ...51

- *Fern, Rick*
THE POWER OF THE WORD 38

- *Gottlieb, Adrienne*
THE HEAD AND NOT THE TAIL 30
CLEAN OR UNCLEAN
CALLED-OUT OR THE SAME 87
IS THE PROPHET AMOS RELEVANT
TODAY? 125

Contents

- *Hicks, Michael*
LET THIS MIND BE IN YOU 21
GOD IS FOR YOU 129

- *Higgins, Bruce A.*
OUR MAIN FOCUS IN LIFE 4
GOD IS YOUR ANSWER; NOT YOUR PROBLEM ...54
STAND UP TO THE DEVIL! 73
JESUS WAS A FRIEND 94
THERE'S A BALANCE—MONEY 128
HE MUST GO THROUH SAMARIA 151
DISTRACTIONS 169
STAY IN THE MIDDLE OF THE ROAD 185

- *Holloman, Daryl P*
BLESSINGS AND SUCCESS 56

- *Howard, William Paul*
OUR GOD INHABITS PRAISE 3
SHEEP CAN BE LED 29
I CAN'T STOP 50
CONSIDERING HER FOR MINISTRY 92
WITH YOU IN MIND 108
I WANTA BE 134
THE SEARCH 171
DO YOU FEEL HIM NOW? 183

- *Jeffries, Rachel*
A BIG CHURCH FIGHT! 31
A CALM MIND AND HEART 83
AN AWAKENING SONG 109
PULLING YOURSELF UP BY THE BOOTSTRAPS 145
WALKING BY FAITH 180

Contents

- *Jones, Aaron*
FREELY GIVE US ALL THINGS 23
A VISION—GOD'S HEALING RIVER 49
THE BATTLE 66
FROM WHERE GOD STANDS 101
NO NEGATIVES 131
AMBASSADORS FOR CHRIST 143
GOD IS STILL SPEAKING TO MEN 175
DILIGENTLY STUDY SHOW GOD
YOUR HEART 189

- *Jones, Lynn Whitlock*
A SOUL DAY 26
ADOPTION 85
HEARTS FOCUS 96
FINE TUNED TO HEAR GOD 123
LISTENING TO GOD 142
PATIENCE 161
TRUST IN THE PROCESS 182

- *Kelley, Ron*
FIRST KNOWING THE GIFTS OF
THE HOLY SPIRIT 63
ANOINTED WORD FOR NOW IN THESE
END TIMES 113
ON THE ROAD AGAIN 167

- *Kirk, Susan E.*
ANSWERED PRAYER 10
HE SENT TWO ANGELS 102
GOD COMPLETES HIS PROMISES 163

Contents

- *Knox, Rhonda*
MOMMA, I'VE FALLEN IN LOVE
WITH PARAGUAY 36

- *Lampkin, Bobby*
THE THREE CROSSES 61

- *Lane III, Roger K.*
YOU CAN'T EVEN SEE IT 8
THE SHEEP ANSWER 80
GOD DOES A WORK AROUND 134
WORSHIP WORDS 170

- *Marr, Ed*
WHY SACKCLOTH AND ASHES? 76
TREES OF RELIGION 118

- *Moore, Bill "Moe"*
IDENTIFYING THE THIEF, THE DESTROYER 19

- *Nokes, Michael*
THE ATTITUDE (HEART) OF THE
GOOD SAMARITAN 15
THE SPIRIT OF JEZEBEL 68
ABOUT BEING LED 114
THE GREATEST SCIENTIST TO EVER LIVE 147
THE LOVE OF MONEY 165
WHY WE SHOULD FOCUS ON THE BEAM 173

- *Ohse, Brian*
WILL YOU PAY THE PRICE 59
WATCH YOUR WALK 187

Contents

- *Ranney, Allen*
VICTORY IN JESUS 6
THE AARONIC BLESSING 81
THE LORD'S PRAYER 137

- *Ranney, Karen*
THE BLESSINGS OF OUR HEALER 45
GOD'S AWESOME PLAN 159

- *Ricker, Doug*
GOD WILL MEET YOUR NEED 41

- *Sanders, LisaMarie*
HIS GREAT LOVE FOR ME 34

- *Sanders, Wayne*
WHO IS THIS JESUS? 78
GOD IS A GOD OF ORDER 122

- *Steinmetz, William J. "Bill"*
WHAT IS TRUTH? 117

- *White, Barbara J.*
PERSISTENCE 43
THE CURE FOR FRETTING 75
THE INCORRUPTIBLE SEED 98
THE FIRE OF THE HOLY SPIRIT............................135
I DON'T DO GRUMPY 155

- *Young, Steve*
NOW IS THE TIME 13
4 STEPS TO FORGIVING OTHERS 111
TIME FOR A HEART CHECK-UP 153

Contents

THE WEAPONS OF OUR WARFARE 192

Authors' Ministry Contact Information 195

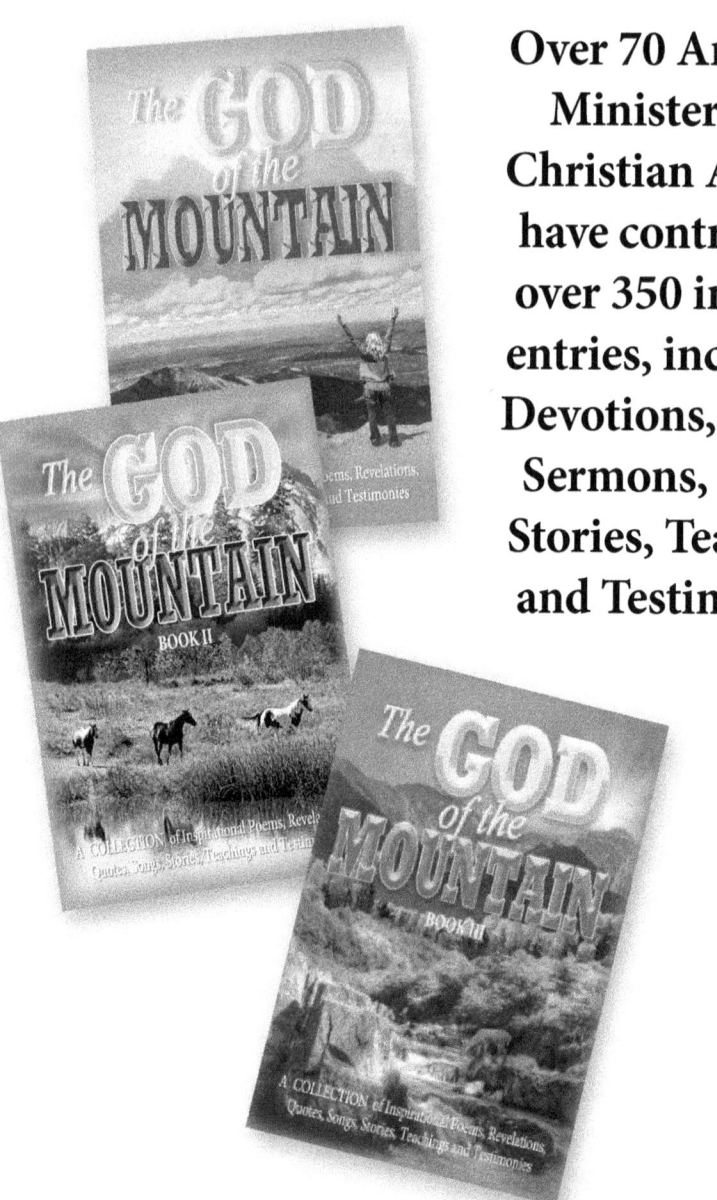

Over 70 Anointed Ministers and Christian Authors have contributed over 350 inspired entries, including: Devotions, Poems, Sermons, Songs, Stories, Teachings and Testimonies.

"Add a shot of God's goodness to your morning coffee break, with 'The GOD of the MOUNTAIN' Series. You will be so blessed you did!"

Available through this ministry and at
AMAZON.COM

Foreword

by Adrienne Gottlieb

The GOD of the MOUNTAIN is a collection of writings from members of the Body of Christ just like you; the reader. Most of us are ordinary people just trying to live out our lives in service to God. We don't have big ministries or mega churches but we have learned so much along the way that we want to share it with you.

Our third volume completes the series and gives the reader a devotional with at least 365 entries. Each entry comes from the heart of a brother or sister in Christ with the hope that as *"iron sharpens iron,"* you will be sharpened as you read. It is our desire that whether it be a single line, several pages or the entire volume that you will be provoked to carry out your calling and God's work as the Body of Christ while we are still on this earth.

As I write this brief Foreword, it is the Jewish New Year (Rosh Hashana) or The Feast of Trumpets. A Feast that the Lord gave us and that few of us pay attention to. Yet one day, in the not too distant future, THE TRUMPET will blow, *the dead in Christ* will arise and along with *those who remain* will meet our Atonement, The Christ (Yom Kippur) and He will Tabernacle (Succoth) among us once again. How glorious is that? Are you ready?

Until that time, we have a duty to share with the world what it means to be THE CHURCH, the Called-out Peo-

Foreword

ple of God. *We are to be the head, not the tail.* We are to set examples for the world to see and follow. We are to *"come out from among them"* and *demonstrate* that we really do have the answers, answers *in love* and not judgment, answers that the world desperately needs.

If only the American Church would dare to separate itself from the world. If 13 men three thousand years ago could change their known world with lasting results three millennia later, how much more the millions who profess to be Christian in America could change our world today. I can't help but wonder, is it that we don't believe, that we fear the world or that we are deceived? Is it that our priorities are with ourselves and not God? Is it that we are just plain lazy and self-absorbed? We love a good sermon. We love to be inspired. We love to be charitable (to a certain extent), but do we truly love Christ? Is He really our Lord? As the saying goes today: Just asking.

As you read, I pray you find new courage to do great things for God. I pray these writings inspire you to witness your faith in Christ, and demonstrate what you and I say we believe—Harvest time is upon us.

We have a long way to go, in a short time. Nevertheless, my prayer is still *"maranatha,"* come Lord Jesus.

Adrienne Gottlieb,
Under the shadow of His Wings.

Acknowledgments

As a Minister of The Gospel and a Publisher, I would like to thank the following people for helping to bring me to this place in my life and ministry, and for helping make this incredible '3 Book Series' possible.

SPECIAL THANKS to (my beautiful wife) Anita Jones; and fellow ministers: George Ballew, Charles England, Pastor Steve Farmer, Daryl Holloman, Jim Isreal, Dr. Rachel Jeffries, Dr. Dave Leggett, Ed Marr, Brian Ohse, Pastors Lionicio & Alma Perez, Dean & Ruth Remmers, Wayne Sanders, Elizabeth Pruitt Sloan, Brad Stine, Pastor Kenn Watson, Kim Wear and (the late Emmett Spencer, Michael Hicks, Ronnie Moore and Rigoberto Perez) for speaking into my life and ministry—you all share in this ministry's eternal rewards.

Again to Daryl Holloman and Jim Isreal, my Board Members, intercessors, and trusted Friends. Much appreciation and love to both of you, without your examples of faith, fellowship, input, prayers and support, none of this would be possible.

A BIG GOD BLESS YOU and THANK YOU to all the Authors that contributed your writings, time, money and prayers into this project. You are all an integral part of God's great mission to the lost and forgotten of this old world. Working together, we are making the GOOD NEWS of God's Son, JESUS CHRIST known in all the Earth.

Acknowledgments

Introduction

I have been a 'paid publisher' for myself and other Christian Authors since January of 2014. God has blessed me in that, as a publisher I get to read everyone's materials (teachings, revelations, testimonies, etc.); and work with some of God's most gifted leadership.

The challenge about leaders is: by their very nature, they are assertive, bold, and strong in their convictions. Someone once said, *"Working with leaders is like trying to herd cats. Every one of them has their own way of doing things."* But I love them, and God has called me and positioned me to work with all of them (the Apostles, Prophets, Evangelists, Pastors and Teachers) as well as those called as: Artists, Authors, Educators, Encouragers, Exhorters, Helps, Poets, Singers and Songwriters.

This Devotional is a testimony to the unifying power of the Holy Ghost of God, [for we are all one Body in Him], and has been brought together, put together and produced under His direction.

In August 2017, Prophet Charles Althouse prophesied to me at a small church just outside of Vinita, Oklahoma:
"Aaron Jones, you about to do a project for God. I don't know why He is calling it a project because it has to do with your publishing company. But I'm hearing you are going to do a project. It's going to bless a lot of people…and it is going to make a lot of money! I mean this thing is going to go, it's going to get big—I'm hear-

Introduction

ing the word 'viral'..., then he kinda laughed and said, "and I don't even know what viral means! But that's what I am hearing, that this thing is going to go viral."

I believe this "GOD of the MOUNTAIN" SERIES OF BOOKS is that project. Thus far, (the first two volumes) the response has been overwhelming, with over 66 different Authors contributing over 240 different inspired writings, and many requesting how to purchase the books even before their completion.

I think I speak for all of the Authors, when I say, *"It is our prayer that you (the reader) receive this book in the same way that it came together—in the spirit of unity and the bond of peace. Believing it will jump start your day with the Lord and be a blessing to you and your family or ministry.*

"Blessings and much love to you in the all-powerful, unmatched Name of God's only Son—Jesus!"

    Sincerely,
    Aaron Jones

The GOD of the MOUNTAIN

BOOK III

In memory of our Friend, Brother and fellow Minister,

Rev. Michael R. Hicks
(June 1958 — March 2020)

We know your faith has ended in sight of His Glory.
We will see you again!

OUR GOD INHABITS PRAISE
by William Paul Howard

How many of you give God praise continually? We are instructed to praise God always. When you get up, then all day long and when you go to sleep at night. Give God praise. Thank Him for the many blessings He has poured out upon you. Yes, even if you are going through a rough spot. When you're up on the mountain top or down in the valley low—give God praise.

I ask my youngest daughter once: When you pray, do you treat God like He's *a genie in a bottle*; rubbing on the bottle and asking for 3 wishes. Her reply was yes. I then ask her if she ever thanked God for the things she needed. You see, when you ask for something in Jesus' Name, go ahead and thank God for the thing you want. Jesus said whatsoever things ye ask for believing, ye shall receive. So if you believe that you're going to recieve what you ask for; then, go ahead and thank Him for it while you are praying. I thank You Lord for the_____. I thank You Lord for my ___. I give You praise. Thank You Lord. Your Word says You will supply all my need and I thank You Lord for supplying them ahead of time. Thank You Lord in Jesus' Name. HALLELUJAH! Praise be to God! Go ahead and thank Him ahead of time, everyday for the things you are believing for. Every time you get a chance. You might want to make a list and as they manifest, you can circle them and give God praise for supplying them and watch your faith grow.

~

OUR MAIN FOCUS IN LIFE
by Bruce A. Higgins

The major goal of any Christian, no matter where you go to church or how long you have walked with God, should be winning the lost. If you don't have a heart to reach someone else with the Good News of Christ, you have missed it. Missed what? You've missed why Jesus came into this world.

> John 10:10 KJV
> The thief cometh not, but for to steal, and to kill, and to destroy: I am come that they might have life, and that they might have [it] more abundantly.

In the Gospels, we see Jesus as Savior, Lord, provider, and teacher; but, in John 4:42 we also see Jesus as a true Friend. We see the Son of the living God leaving the glory of Heaven to come to Earth, to be born of a virgin, grow up, enter the ministry, and then die for the sins of the entire world.

Often overlooked in all of this great plan of God, is the fact that He was led of the Holy Spirit to go to Samaria to touch one woman's life in a way she was never touched before.

TOUCHING PEOPLE'S LIVES

Touching other people's lives should be the main focus for believers. That's what Jesus taught and that's what Jesus did. Jesus gave His life for others.

There was Jesus reaching out to one desperate woman in the heat of the day. Isn't that just like the God we serve? He tells us to go and do likewise.

> Mark 16:15 KJV
> And he said unto them, Go ye into all the world, and preach the gospel to every creature.

∽

GOD IS ON YOUR SIDE
by Ginny Bridges

GOD IS ON YOUR SIDE — Just want to remind you that if the devil didn't give it to you, he can't take it away from you. Whether it's a home, health, finances, a job, a relationship, peaceful sleep … whatever it is … if you received it as a blessing from God, then stand your ground and don't let the enemy of your soul take it from you. If the rumor is that these blessings are in jeopardy, but God's promised to provide, then decide who you're going to believe and stick with it. Hold up your *shield of faith* against those fiery darts of fear and worry, and confidently face the day, knowing Whose you are. Remember, God is on your side!

VICTORY IN JESUS
by Allen Ranney

Victory in Jesus, what a beautiful old song.

"Victory in Jesus, my Savior forever, He sought me and bought me, with His redeeming blood."

Have you ever thought about it though?

What is victory in Jesus to you?

Maybe that we're going to go to Heaven one day? That's nice, or may be John 3:16 comes to mind, very good. But, have you ever really thought about it? I have and Scripture is rife with word illustrations, starting of course in the Old Testament.

2 Samuel 23:12 reads, "But he stationed himself in the middle of the field, defended it, and killed the Philistines. So, the Lord brought about a great victory."

Victory is a military term, it is defined as:

1. Final and complete supremacy or superiority in battle or war.
2. A specific military engagement ending in triumph.
3. Success in any contest or struggle involving the defeat of an opponent/enemy or overcoming obstacles.

The Strong's Concordance reference number for the Hebrew word used as *"salvation"*, is #3467 יֵשׁוּעַ *Yeshua*, which has been translated in Greek as: Jesus.

The Name of Jesus, in Hebrew is *Yeshua*. Jesus in English is a nice enough Name, but it really doesn't convey much meaning. Yeshua, however means "He is our salvation."

Does anyone know the Hebrew word for *"victory"*? It is *yesha* #3467 יֶשַׁע, and yesha is the root word in Yeshua, so, you can see and hear from the very letters of the word that there is "victory in Yeshua" Hallelujah! Victory in Jesus, yesha! Yeshua Messiah yesha! Victory in Jesus.

Jesus is our victory as He has already conquered death and Hell. Amen.

Revelation 1:18 reads, "I am He who lives, and was dead, and behold, I am alive forevermore. Amen and I have the keys of hell and of death."

Other names for Jesus/Yeshua Messiah are militaristic in their origin.

Commander/Captain/Prince #8267 שַׂר Sar– Joshua 5:14 reads, "and He said, Nay; but as Captain of the host of the Lord am I now come. And Joshua fell on his face to the earth, and did worship, and said unto Him, what sayeth my Lord unto His servant.

Deliverer/Redeemer #1350 גאל *Goel* – Romans 11:26 reads, "And so all Israel will be saved, as it is written: The Deliverer will come out of Zion and He will turn away ungodliness from Jacob; for this is My covenant with them, when I take away their sins." (Isaiah 59:20)

Scepter #7626 שבט Shebet – Numbers 24:17 reads, "There shall come a Star out of Jacob, and a Scepter shall rise out of Israel, and shall smite the corners of Moab, and destroy all the children of Sheth.

This should bring great comfort to any believer as we are encouraged in Romans 8:37 – 39, "Yet in all these things *we are more than conquerors* through Him who loved us. For I am persuaded that neither death nor life, nor angels nor principalities nor powers, nor things present nor things to come, nor height nor depth, nor any other created thing, shall be able to separate us from the love of God which is in Christ Jesus our Lord. Amen. Now that's Victory in Jesus!

YOU CAN'T EVEN SEE IT
by Roger K. Lane III

Summer 1992, I left Kenneth Hagin's night service early from downtown Tulsa. I wanted to miss the traffic and see Mom and Dad before they went to bed. My little, black,

1984 Fiero was parked in the Double Tree's multi-level garage across the street. Having grown up in this part of Tulsa, I knew there were several ways to get to their house from here. 16th and Peoria was only two miles away. I thought, you know, I think I'll take 18th street.

Arriving at my car, I needed to get moving to miss the traffic. Backing out, I was startled by the sensation of someone or something pushing my car on the left. I looked and no-one was there. My Fiero moved towards the car on my right. The side mirror barely touched the neighboring vehicle. Able to maneuver away, not touching the car again, thinking, "wow that was weird." I got out and looked and to my surprise there was no mark left.

Shaking my head, I walked back to my vehicle, wondering what just happened. Sitting down the Holy Spirit spoke to me real big on the inside. *"Get out a business card and put an arrow on it with a note saying I scratched your car. I'm sorry. Please call."* Saying with assertiveness *"Lord You can't even see it!"* We went back and forth with this conversation a few times. Finally, I got out, went over and pressed my card with the note between the driver's glass and rubber, placing it arrow down, approximately where the mirror had made contact.

Grateful to be leaving, I proceeded with a direct route coming to a stop at the 18th and Peoria intersection facing East. Looking both directions there were no cars in sight. I was getting ready to ease onto Peoria when one came flying over the small hill to the North headed South. Slamming on my brakes, sparks flew from what looked like a rocket as the flying projectile bottomed out just past the hill in the divot we all avoided. It was traveling over a hundred miles per hour as it screamed passed the front of my Fiero (a Pontiac that was made out of some kind of plastic). Behind this comet was a policeman right on his tail, his vehicle traveling at the speed it chased! It was only seconds for all this to flash before me. Seconds that found my heart in my throat. Again the Lord spoke up real loud on the inside, *"Had you not done what I asked in the parking garage, you would have been in the middle of the road and met Me in Heaven."*

Hebrews 1:14
Are they not all ministering spirits, sent forth to minister for them who shall be heirs of salvation?

ANSWERED PRAYER
by Susan E. Kirk

Matthew 21:22
If you believe, you will receive whatever you ask for in prayer.

I was a new believer. I believed that God was calling me to Mexico. Now, twenty years later, God reminds me of His continuing presence in my life. I am reminded daily of His promises—and God completes His promises!

It was my second time driving to Mexico as an independent Missionary. I was met with a few challenges to my belief in God answering prayers.

I invited Shelly (70ish), John (as my interpreter) and pastor Cesar (also bilingual). John brought his son (age 10) and father (70ish, Wayne). We were taking supplies for ministry, so we drove two vehicles. We were cleared with visas and permissions. I tried to get John to ride with me; so that, there would be an interpreter in each vehicle, but he refused. We began bilinguals in one vehicle, English only in my vehicle. We were scheduled to arrive in Allende at 7pm for supper at the church.

It was dark and rainy. Cesar passed a truck. When I finally passed the truck, Cesar was nowhere in sight. We continued driving. I finally told Shelly and Wayne that we were lost. It was approximately 9pm. We had no cell phones. There was no traffic. We were in the middle of nowhere in Mexico lost. I pulled over to the side of the road and asked Shelly and Wayne to pray for a police officer. Immediately, I was met with opposition. They proceeded to tell me how bad Mexico's police officers were. I said, *"Just pray believing that God will bring good ones."*

I began driving. We made a curve and voila, a police car was on the side of the road. I pulled over. I gathered a notebook, pen, and Spanish-English dictionary. I went over to the police car. One of the officers got out. We were standing in the rain. He began to speak. I tried to write some of the words and look them up in the dictionary. He finally understood that I was trying to get to Montemorelos. The other officer came over. I was standing in the rain, soaking wet, not knowing whether to cry, run, or cry and run. I stood paralyzed. The second officer took my notebook and pen. My heart was racing but my body remained paralyzed. The first officer gently nudged me toward my vehicle. I sat in my vehicle near tears and silent.

The officers began walking toward my vehicle, so I met them. The second officer handed me back my notebook with a map complete with road marks along the way. I tried to thank them by telling them that they were angels sent by God. I was pointing to the heavens. They said, "no, somos malos." Later, I understood this statement.

The night is not over, and tomorrow—Encounter II.

Today, focus on God's promises. God completes His promises. God answered my prayer according to Matthew 21:22. God answered His promise to provide according to Matthew 7:11 and 2 Corinthians 9:8-11. God answered His promise to protect according to 2 Thessalonians 3:3. All were answered in the form of Mexican police officers who knew how to give directions.

God revealed His promises to me that dark and rainy

night in nowhere Mexico. Where and when has He revealed His promises to you? Remember them, all of them, and give God thanks daily for His promises.

NOW IS THE TIME
by Steve Young

We are currently experiencing and living in a time where people are so easily offended by any type of disagreement, i.e., their beliefs, actions, lifestyles or political affiliations, etc. Because of these disagreements, acts of violence, rebellion, racial slurs, name-calling, along with demonstrations and riotous protests have become stronger and almost a daily occurrence. All this hate, temper, abuse, bitterness, and unforgiveness has generated to the point where it has become acceptable.

Now is the time for Christians to step up and be stronger in displaying the Word of God with our deeds of expressing Christ's love through us toward others. Now is the time to remind our countrymen of the principles that our country was first founded on. Now is the time to express love and forgiveness toward one another:

> Ephesians 5:2a AMPC
> "And walk in love, [esteeming and delighting in one another] as Christ loved us and gave Himself up for us…"

Forgiving others who have hurt you, wronged you, badgered you, and crushed your inner feelings, reputation, trust, dignity, and self-esteem is most likely the most difficult thing you will ever attempt. However, it's 'a must' thing to do, to keep from destroying yourself. Author Lewis Smedes once wrote, "To forgive is to set a prisoner free and discover that the prisoner was you."

We are instructed by The Apostle Paul, "Let all bitterness and indignation and wrath [passion, rage, bad temper] and resentment [anger, animosity] and quarreling [brawling, clamor, contention] and slander [evil speaking, abusive or blasphemous language] be banished from you, with all malice [spite, ill will, or baseness of any kind]. And become useful and helpful and kind to one another, tenderhearted [compassionate, understanding, lovinghearted], forgiving one another [readily and freely], as God in Christ forgave you." (Ephesians 4:31-31 AMP)

Are you having difficulty in knowing how or where to start forgiving those who have caused your hurts and offenses in the past? Now is the time to begin by going to our Heavenly Father, the omniscient One Who knows and sees ALL of your hurts and pains. Through the blood of Jesus Christ, He forgave you. Therefore, seek Him and ask Him to give you the strength you need, to guide you in His direction, and help you move forward by giving you a heart of forgiveness. NOW IS THE TIME!

THE ATTITUDE (HEART) OF THE GOOD SAMARITAN
by Michael Nokes

A couple of months ago, I fell on roller skates celebrating a little girl's birthday. As I fell I heard the bones break; my wrist was severely misshapen so I covered it with my other hand. Immediately I was asked, "Is it broken"? I replied, "Yes" but I shouldn't have. Although within seconds, God showed me that He was going to use it to show me great things. I began to thank God. Not for the break, but because of what He allowed me to see in that moment.

In the days following a strange thing happened to me. I had just paid some large sums of money out and I found myself in dire need. Contrary to the worldly thought process, I had peace. Yet as I went through my options I discovered a perfect storm had occurred and I didn't have anything available. I was in real need, emergency need!

One day as I was reaching out for help from my brethren, I saw in the spirit, the road described in the Bible and the dying man in need of help. As the priest and the Levite walked by, one very fast, and the other thinking; but then, not stopping, I saw Jesus looking out of the eyes of the man suffering on the roadside. Then I saw and felt Jesus' appreciation when the Good Samaritan stopped and the dying man was SURE of help. And I realized the depth of which Jesus' *message of compassion* was supposed to have taught me to love my neighbor and my brethren.

Allow the lesson of the Good Samaritan in Luke 10:33-36 (KJV) to change you: 33 But a certain Samaritan, as he journeyed, came where he was: and when he saw him, he had COMPASSION on him, 34 And went to him, and bound up his wounds, pouring in oil and wine, and set him on his own beast, and brought him to an inn, and took CARE of him. 35 And on the morrow when he departed, HE TOOK OUT TWO PENCE, AND GAVE them to the host, and said unto him, Take CARE of him; and whatsoever thou spendest more, when I come again, I WILL REPAY thee. 36 Which now of these three, thinkest thou, was NEIGHBOUR unto him that fell among the thieves?

Then in Matthew 25:40-41 (KJV), we see our Shepherd dividing His Sheep from the goats.

> 40 And the King shall answer and say unto them, Verily I say unto you, INASMUCH AS YE HAVE DONE IT UNTO one of the least of these MY BRETHREN, YE HAVE DONE IT UNTO ME.
> 41 Then shall he say also unto them on the left hand, Depart from me, ye cursed, into everlasting fire, prepared for the devil and his angels:

The attitude of our Lord is described in Proverbs 19:17 and

again in Matthew 5:42. His promise is in Psalm 37:25-26 and it's all summed up in Matthew 7:12; Jesus will repay.

SINGLE & TRUSTING GOD FOR A MATE
by Sharon Andrews

Isaiah 34:16b NKJV
Not one of these shall fail; Not one shall lack her mate. For My mouth has commanded it, and His Spirit has gathered them.

Psalm 37:4 KJV
Delight thyself also in the LORD; and he shall give thee the desires of thine heart.

I was ministering and seeking first the Kingdom of God, while trusting God for a mate. I wanted God's choice for a mate. I had gone to Bible College and and met a man that was from the same state as me, with the same calling. I was engaged to him while in school. I continued to make sure I was making the right decision, continually seeking the Lord.

I began to notice some areas of his character that troubled me. I broke up with him.

I found out later that a woman in class with me began to pray for me. The Holy Spirit had directed her to pray for me concerning a mate. She then asked a friend to pray for me and see if the Lord showed her anything. She told her I was about to marry the wrong person. They wanted to tell me, but the Holy Spirit directed them not to tell me, they were told I wasn't going to miss God, because I was seeking Him.

It looked like I was going to miss it. I thank God, that He raised up intercessors to pray for me, so that I would make the right choice for a mate. I had broken up with him, because I continued to seek God's plan for my life, and they prayed for me.

I didn't date; instead, I allowed the Holy Spirit to direct me to who He wanted me to fellowship with. I learned to guard my heart, so as not to get hurt.

1 Samuel 16:10-13 became my pattern to receive the promise of a mate. David was chosen as King from among the seven sons of Jesse. All the other sons passed by, but David was chosen as King. *Man looks on the outward appearance, but God looks on the heart.* I was instructed that many men would pass by, but that I would know God's choice for my mate. My eyes were not on a mate, but on doing the will of God and that He would add the promise. I knew I would be at the right place at the right time, to meet the right man.

One day, while at church I was approached by a woman that was wanting to know if the man she was dating was the right one for her. I told her: when in doubt—don't! A well dressed man came through the church entrance. I pointed to him and said, "Now that's the kind of man I would want to marry." She said, "That's him!" I pointed to him by the Holy Spirit and had never done anything like that before. The man she was dating and questioning about, the one I pointed to would end up being my husband, Jim.

God was faithful to send His choice for a mate. I was directed by the Holy Spirit, seeking first the Kingdom—not a mate.

Jim had prayed for a mate and had a vsion of him and his wife mnistering together. He saw in the vision that one would minister and then the other. And this is exactly how we minister—together.

We've now been married over 30 years, and minister as:
A TEAM.

IDENTIFYING THE THIEF, THE DESTROYER
by Bill "Moe" Moore

We've all attempted to console, minister, and sympathize with family and friends who have experienced devastating loss, sorrow or even death.

On more than one occasion, I've had the misfortune to hear people immediately blame God, and not identify the true culprit: *satan*.

Jesus told us in John 10:10 emphatically it's *the thief* (satan/lucifer/devil) that comes to steal, kill, & destroy.

Blaming God is easier, I understand. But, it's the WRONG DECISION for anyone to make!

For in the same verses, Jesus said He came to bless each of us with an abundant life, full of blessings!

Nowhere in the New Testament (Covenant) does God's Word authorize any murdering! How in the world can Jesus go against His Father's Word, and kill, steal, or destroy anyone? That would be contrary to the *grace and mercy* taught throughout the New Testament, mostly by Jesus, the Son of God!

Jesus is the epitomized picture of *love*; therefore, malice, murder, and mayhem is not in Him! Those are unallowable by God!

Instead, give Him praise in your dire straits! He deserves the glory!

> *John 10:10*
> *For the thief comes to kill, steal, & destroy. But I came to give life more abundantly!*

NOTE: Jesus is NOT your adversary, but rather *He is your Advocate in Love, Peace, Joy,* and *Hope*

LET THIS MIND BE IN YOU
by Michael R. Hicks

Jesus did not step out of eternity onto Earth just to save us from our sins. He did not come to earth just to give us life and life more abundantly. Indeed, Jesus accomplished all these things. All of these are important because it is the plan of God and His plan hasn't changed. The reason Jesus came was to give us the blue print for life, ministry, and eternal life. He came to give us the recipe for Godly living. And He started teaching us God's blueprint by being an example for us.

> Philippians 2:5-8
> 5 Let this mind be in you which was also in Christ Jesus,
> 6 Who being in the form of God; did not consider it robbery to be equal with God:
> 7 But made Himself of no reputation, taking the form of a bondservant, and coming in the likeness of men.
> 8 And being found in appearance as a man, He humbled Himself and became obedient to the point of death, even death of the cross.

All godly actions begin with the *renewing of the mind.* We renew our mind by meditating and rolling the instructions of Christ over and over in our minds until it becomes alive in our spirits. The Word of God strengthens believers into thinking good or right thoughts. Right thinking produces right actions. Bad thinking or stinking thinking produces bad actions. The actions of believers are the fruits of our deepest thoughts. God is the Author of our deepest thoughts and He lines us up with divine appointments in order for us to bear good fruit. The more we meditate on the Word of God, the more sensitive we become to His Voice, and the stronger we become in Christ Jesus. We also become useful as Kingdom builders for Him. Thinking and being like Christ are requirements for believers. If we are not thinking and living as Christ, then we need to examine our relationship, repent and yield to Him so that we may be strengthened and get back on the right track. As the Body of Christ, we need to think and act like one being, because Jesus the Christ, God the Father and God the Holy Spirit are—ONE.

> Philippians 2:5-7 AMP
> 5 Have this same attitude in yourselves which was in Christ Jesus [look to Him as your example in selfless humility],
> 6 who, although He existed in the form and unchanging essence of God [as One with Him, possessing the fullness of all the divine attributes—the entire nature of deity], did not regard equality with God a thing to be grasped or asserted [as if He did not already possess it, or was afraid of losing it];
> 7 but emptied Himself [without renouncing or diminishing His deity, but only temporarily giving up the outward expression of divine equality and His rightful dignity] by assuming the form of a bond-

servant, and being made in the likeness of men [He became completely human but was without sin, being fully God and fully man].

Since Christ is God the Son, it did not bother Him or trouble Him sharing His Father's nature because God the Father, God the Son, and God the Holy Ghost are One. He was already God the Son, full of everything that God is. But Jesus didn't trip, ponder, contemplate, or think it over; He made Himself of no reputation, He just emptied Himself of His godly (or God-like) power and came to Earth as a mere man.

Jesus came to Earth as the *son of man*, so that we may one day return to Heaven as—THE SONS OF GOD.

FREELY GIVE US ALL THINGS
by Aaron Jones

We must get settled on this TRUTH:

> Romans 8:32 KJV (italics mine)
> He that spared not his own Son, but delivered him up for us all, how shall he not with him *also freely give us all things*?

Understand that God has already given Heaven's best, His only Son—JESUS. If He was going to tell us "No" on any request, this would have been the one. If He was going to deny us anything, He's already missed His chance [2,000 years ago] when He gave us Jesus, raised Him from the dead and sent the Holy Ghost. Now all of His promises are not set in stone. No....it's way better than that---His promises are set in His Word! That He said were YES and AMEN, and that they would *never pass away*. (cf. 2 Co 1:20)

If God doesn't want me healed, then He shouldn't have..

If God doesn't want me blessed, then He shouldn't have!

Telling me (promising) that: all things are possible to him that believeth. (See: Mk 9:23)

> John 14:13-14 NKJV
> 13 "And whatever you ask in My name, that I will do, that the Father may be glorified in the Son.
> 14 "If you ask anything in My name, I will do [it].
>
> Mark 11:24 KJV
> Therefore I say unto you, What things soever ye desire, when ye pray, believe that ye receive [them], and ye shall have [them].

In those last hours of battle and agony, from the garden to the tomb, Jesus paved the way (if you can receive it) for —you and I to win in every area of life.

- He took on every sin, evil, effect of darkness and unrighteous act; so that, you and I can walk in the light; in complete righteousness.

▪ He took on every sickness, pain and disease ever known or experienced; so that you and I can be completely healed and whole. (cf. 1 Pe 2:24)

▪ He became poor, (stripped down to nothing) so that you and I can be rich! (cf. Deu 8:18; 2 Co 8:9; Ga 3:29)

▪ He stepped over into Death and spent 3 days in Hell; so that you and I can have life in abundance (See: Jo 10:10) and live out His will down here, like it is up there—LIKE THE DAYS OF HEAVEN ON EARTH. (cf. Mt 6:10; Lk 11:2; Deu 11:21)

We are <u>complete in Him</u>.
<u>The head</u> and not the tail,
<u>Above only</u> and not beneath,
<u>The lender</u> and not the borrower,
<u>Having all sufficiency</u> in all things,
<u>Abounding to</u> every good work,
<u>in abundance</u>,
<u>in authority</u>,
<u>Kings and priests</u> unto God,
<u>Seated in heavenly places</u>,
<u>Reigning and ruling with Him</u>!!!

A SOUL DAY
by Lynn Whitlock Jones

Have you not known? Have you not heard? The everlasting God, the Lord , The Creator of the ends of the earth, Neither faints nor is weary. His understanding is unsearchable. He gives power to the weak, And to those who have no might He increases strength. Even the youths shall faint and be weary, And the young men shall utterly fall, But those who wait on the Lord Shall renew their strength; They shall mount up with wings like eagles, They shall run and not be weary, They shall walk and not faint.
– Isaiah 40:28-31 NKJV

Yesterday was what I call a soul day. My body ached and I was tired. My heart was hurting for many family and friends who have had loved ones battling sickness, disease and death. And I struggled with emotions that would have caused depression had I let them.

I share my struggle, not for sympathy but in the hope that it will help someone else.

We have been fighting many spiritual attacks by praying and standing on the Word of God. And as a believer and a prayer warrior, if I were to allow it, the fight could overwhelm me. However, I chose to overcome this.

I searched for those Scriptures in Psalms where David wrote of his heartfelt emotions and his exuberant expressions of God's grace, mercy, greatness and faithfulness. David knew that in the lowest times and in his every battle; God's presence and promises would enable him to press through adversity to victory.

And as Holy Spirit ministered to me through these Words I realized that I too can write of God's grace, mercy and greatness evident in my life! I know that He is with me and His promises are my victory.

Then Holy Spirit reminded me of this passage from Isaiah. As I read it, I was reminded of the fact that God does not grow weary, He does not give up. And He is the ruler of all! He understands all things, even the things we struggle to understand. Yet, He still gives us strength and power to overcome and soar!

I chose to rest in Him and allow Him to *renew my strength*, to renew my ability to *run the race* and *fight the good fight of faith*. I choose to trust, believe and hold onto my confident expectation that God is and He will always be faithful.

And this morning, after resting in Him, I am renewed and ready to soar! I pray that you too can take comfort and get strength from God's presence and His Word. Choose to rest in His peace, be renewed and then soar like He created you to soar!

AN AMAZING MIRACLE
by Marty Clancy

Hebrews 2:4 says "God also bearing witness both with *signs and wonders, with various miracles*, and gifts of the Holy Spirit, according to His own will."

In the 1980's we traveled with our two small children and ministered throughout the United States. One Sunday night as I was preaching at a church in Georgia, the Holy Spirit kept interrupting me. I was preaching about the goodness of God. I began to say, *"God is good and it's going to rain in Georgia."* I was more bold as the service continued and said, *"Even if every weatherman says there'll be no rain, I'm telling you it's going to rain in Georgia; furthermore, every place in the U.S. that needs rain— it's going to rain."* We had heard that Georgia was experiencing a serious drought with no rain in the forecast.

The service ended with people responding for salvation, coming back to Jesus, the baptism in the Holy Spirit and prayer for healing. As we finished loading our station wagon with our sound equipment and were saying goodbye to the Pastor, it began to rain! The timing was amazing to say the least.

It continued to rain all night. Georgia got 8 inches! In the morning we heard on TV that it was raining all over the

United States where they needed rain. We drove home that day in the rain, rejoicing in *the power of God* who never stops proving His greatness to those who believe.

SHEEP CAN BE LED
by William Paul Howard

In the 23rd Psalm, it says: He leadeth me beside the still waters. Sheep can be led. Goats cannot, they have to be pulled or carried.. God has good things in store for His sheep who can be led. You're given a free will. God will not force you to take the blessings He has for you. He will not grab you by the horns and pull you to them. He will lead you to the waters and the green grass, and there—YOU SHALL NOT WANT.

> Psalm 23:1-6 KJV
> 1 [[A Psalm of David.]] The LORD [is] my shepherd; I shall not want.
> 2 He maketh me to lie down in green pastures: he leadeth me beside the still waters.
> 3 He restoreth my soul: he leadeth me in the paths of righteousness for his name's sake.
> 4 Yea, though I walk through the valley of the shadow of death, I will fear no evil: for thou [art] with me; thy rod and thy staff they comfort me.
> 5 Thou preparest a table before me in the presence of mine enemies: thou anointest my head with oil; my cup runneth over.

6 Surely goodness and mercy shall follow me all the days of my life: and I will dwell in the house of the LORD for ever.

∽

THE HEAD AND NOT THE TAIL
by Adrienne Gottlieb

The powers of darkness are not meant to be left alone. They are to be confronted. When we see evil wreaking havoc, we are not meant to run from it; but rather, we are meant to run toward it. As Christians we were created to do *warfare* with the enemy of humankind.

When God led the Israelites into the Promised Land, he left enemies there that his people had to face. Why? He intended his people to do warfare. No human being anywhere on Earth is left un-harassed by Satan. And if we're not engaged in warfare with him, we're being beaten up by him!

The good news is, we've been given weapons for this warfare, and they are not carnal (2 Cor 10:4). Psalm 144:1 states: Blessed be the LORD, my rock, Who trains my hands for war, And my fingers for battle. Our weapons are found in Christ—and He won every battle He ever faced. He says we can do the same. "Yet in all these things *we are more than conquerors through Him* who loved us" (Rom 8:37).

As Christians, we are in *a spiritual battle* of some sort on a daily basis. In warfare, battles are fought on different fronts, for different reasons, and with varying degrees of intensity. The same is true in spiritual warfare. Our spiritual battles and warfare are real, even though we cannot physically see the attacker. But, we can educate ourselves on how the battles are fought and how they impact our lives on a daily basis.

Keith Green, a Christian song writer, wrote, *"I [Satan] used to have to sneak around. But now they just open their doors. No one's looking for my tricks because no one believes in me any more."*

If we choose to ignore or not believe in the spiritual realm, we will find ourselves confused, frustrated, and quenching the peace that God has promised to each of us. The best defense is a strong offense. Just educating ourselves about the spiritual realm is half the fight and God gives us everything else we need to be victorious with the other half.

Jesus promised us an abundant life that starts here on earth. Until we understand the forces that are against us, and are prepared to fight for what is rightfully ours, we will not be able to receive all that God has for us.

A BIG CHURCH FIGHT!
by Rachel V. Jeffries

A big fight in the New Testament came about because of widows. They were murmuring about the widows because this one group was neglected. The disciples got together and decided to have deacons who were anointed to take care of the widows. This was a great job as it gave those called to preach and teach the Word of God the opportunity to put their whole lives into prayer. Thank God they had the godly wisdom to fix this situation.

> Acts 6:1
> And in those days, when the number of the disciples was multiplied, there arose a murmuring of the Grecians against the Hebrews, because their widows were neglected in the daily ministration.

BEING IN A GREAT POSITION

Then my thoughts went to the widows who could be available to pray in revival. I know myself since I have been a widow, I have given myself much more to prayer. I believe we are a special group who can *birth revival* in this hour in our nation. We need to tap into the power of the Holy Spirit to birth things in the earth. We all need our own *war room*. If it is your whole house that is given to prayer that is great too. In a house we owned before my husband's death I had a room set aside for prayer.

MY WAR ROOM

People would come to visit, and they could feel the power of God in that room. Several fell out under the power of God as they entered. Why? It was not because of me, but because God's presence was honored there. Many natural needs can try to keep us out of prayer. We need to give prayer and the Word first place. We are in a great position to birth great things. What a fulfilling life to have—A LIFE OF PRAYER!

<u>Prayer</u>: Father I yield myself to You to pray out Your plans and purposes. I come to You expecting Your power and Your ability to save, heal and restore. Make me a vessel of honor that I may bring glory to Your Name. Make my very being a room for Your presence. Anoint me to pray out things that will bring glory to You. AMEN!

<u>Confession</u>: I am a prayer warrior. I am a miracle going somewhere to happen. God has filled me up with His presence and I make changes everywhere I go. I lay hands on the sick, I cast out devils, I pray with power. I am effective for the Kingdom of God! HALELLUJAH!

LOVE LIFTED ME
by Marcella Burnes

Hurricane upon the sea
Ship tossed to and fro
Needing to bend a knee.

The Spirit bids "come "
The flesh says, "run"
Oh which one, which one?

Never a rare opportune missed

The GOD of the MOUNTAIN III

She crawls upon this ship.
Walking forward under heave and ho,
Right to the Master she does go.

Blessed Master she does cry
Help me quick, before I die
Take the helm of this ship
Turn it, Turn it—Turn it quick

"And *The Master of the sea*
Heard her despairing cry
From the waters lifted she
Now safe am I"

"Love lifted me
Love lifted me
When nothing else could help.
Love lifted Me!"

HIS GREAT LOVE FOR ME
by LisaMarie Sanders

Growing up as a child I fell prey to the plot of the enemy through physical, mental, emotional and other forms of child abuse. Every time I was beaten, I was forcefully told that God hated me and that if this person did not see me do something during the day that God did, then He would kill me in my sleep. Let's face it we are not perfect, and as a child I would "mess up" from time to time and I always felt such condemnation for the simplest of infraction. I never slept as a child, because I was so fearful over this "god" that would kill me in my sleep.

Until one night in the early morning hours *a still small Voice* started to speak to me. He told me He loved me so much that His one and only Son died in my place for my sins and that He would never harm me. This "Voice" would *comfort* me, *encourage* me, and *love* me more than I had ever known.

One day I went to Church with some friends in the neighborhood and saw a picture of Jesus smiling, I knew in an instant that that was a picture of my secret friend, my "Voice". I learned all about His great love and sacrifice for me and how He truly did die in my place. At age ten with tears streaming down my face and my heart so heavily burdened I gave my life to Jesus! I accepted His extravagant gift of His eternal salvation.

Did my life magically improve? No, in fact it grew worse for me and I was thrust into the world at age thirteen, but I was never alone, as Jesus has always walked beside me and He has saved me time and time again. Through many dangers, toils, and snares I have already come, but the Lord delivered me from them all.

Do you know Him? He knew me long before I heard His still small Voice in the middle of the night and He knows you too. Perhaps you too need to feel the peace of a loving Savior Who wants to comfort you and give you peace. *"Come to Me, all you who labor and are heavy laden, and I will give you rest."* (Matthew 11:28)

One of my favorite memories as a child was when my Sunday School teacher, Miss Karen, gave me a brand new Bible with my name on it. I was so excited and happy to learn more about Jesus. The very first Bible verses I memorized were John 3:16-17.

> For God so Loved the world that He gave His only begotten Son, that whosoever believes in Him will not perish but everlasting life. For God did not send His Son into the world to condemn the world but that through Him the world might be saved.

I learned not to accept the lie of the enemy that God hated me, but rather I chose to accept THE TRUTH of God's Word that declares His great love for me!

"Oh, how I love Jesus, because He first loved me."

"MOMMA, I'VE FALLEN IN LOVE WITH PARAGUAY"
by Rhonda Knox

God warns us in dreams, corrects us, gives us direction, teaches us, gives us hope and even pushes us to do something. Have you ever thought about this? God trusted a dreamer to raise His Son, Jesus.

Yes, Joseph was a dreamer. Read Matthew chapter one and two for yourself. God warned Joseph, corrected him, gave him direction, and hope, and taught him many things. Joseph trusted that God spoke to him in his dreams. Joseph saved the life of their son, Jesus, because he knew God spoke to him in dreams.

On June 13, 2014 I went to bed and told God, *"I'm losing hope."* In the night I had a dream from God. He spoke to me a name I had never heard of: Paraguay. When I woke up, I asked my husband, David, if there was a city in the USA called Paraguay. He said, *"No, but there is a country called Paraguay."* I said, *"Well, I need to get there quick!"* I said, *"Someone is losing hope, and I have to find them."* David said, *"Rhonda, we can't go to Paraguay. We don't know a soul in Paraguay."* *"In fact,"* he said, *"We don't know a single person in all of South America."* I said, *"You don't have to go, but I've got to."* I said, *"If Corrie ten Boom can trust that God told her to fly to South America then so can I."* I knew without a doubt that it was a dream from God. We had to take the first step. Two months later, our plane was landing in Paraguay. As I looked out the window, I heard God speak to me. He said, *"Thank you for trusting me."* Now, five years later, we have made five trips to Paraguay. The couple we took with us in 2014 moved to Paraguay to work with the unreached people group called the Guarani Tribe. They moved there five weeks later after we returned from Paraguay that year.

We have helped build five little churches in villages where there were none. They are seeing hundreds come to Jesus where there were no Christians. What we saw in 2014 was breathtaking. Everywhere we went people were losing hope.

The story was so unbelievable that I wrote a book when we returned home titled, **"Momma, I've fallen in love with Paraguay."** Whatever God is asking you to do, do it. As crazy as it might sound—JUST DO IT!

∼

THE POWER OF THE WORD
by Rick Fern

The Word is important. Nothing on Earth has the power that the Word of God has. We, who are Born Again have access to this Miracle-Working, Life-Changing Power. This is a [present day] reality. God *has spoken* and *continues to speak* to us through His Word. His Word has the anointing to accomplish what God desires. We, who Believe have access to that Anointing. *The anointing* is the miracle-working power of God.

God said: "So shall my word be that goeth forth out of my mouth: it shall not return unto me void, but it shall 'accomplish' (the Hebrew word *[asah]* to do or to make; to create) that which I please and it shall prosper in the thing whereto I sent it..." — Isaiah 55:11

When God sends His Word out it brings something back. When YOU send His Word out in faith, it brings something back. He is sending God's Word as a Carrier. It Carries stuff. It brings things in and it takes things out. God's Word will never "not do" something... it—ACCOMPLISHES (creates, makes, does; it *[asah's]*).

God's Word will accomplish what pleases God. What is it that pleases God? Jesus said:

> Luke 12:32
> "Fear not little flock; for it is your Father's good pleasure to give you the Kingdom..."

God wants to GIVE YOU the Kingdom. God is a giving God and it is His giving that brings Him pleasure.

Notice:

1. Faith comes by the Word; therefore, Faith is dependent on the Word.

2. God is revealed by and through the Word.

3. Sinners are Born Again by the Word.

4. Saints have their minds renewed by the Word.

5. Believers are Sanctified by the Word.

6. The Body of Christ is chastened by the Word.

7. The human spirit is recreated by the Word.

8. The Word overcomes the devil and Hell.

9. The Word working in us makes us like Jesus.

The Bible tells us that the Word is Alive and full of Power.

> Hebrews 4:12
> For the word of God is quick, and powerful, and sharper than any two-edged sword, piercing even to the dividing asunder of soul and spirit, and of the joints and marrow, and is a discerner of the thoughts and intents of the heart.

The Word is alive. The Word is loaded and ready to produce. The Word has Heaven-Potential in it. Whatever is in Heaven is in the Word. There is Life in the Word. There is Healing in the Word. There is deliverance in the Word. There is prosperity in the Word. The Word is God.

When it is believed and spoken with the mouth, in faith, it will produce what God produces. There are no restrictions in the Word... nothing is held back that is good.

> Psalm 84:11
> "For the Lord God is a sun and shield: the Lord will give grace and glory: no good thing will He withhold from them that walk uprightly..."

The GOD of the MOUNTAIN III

GOD WILL MEET YOUR NEED
by Doug Ricker

How many times have you thought to yourself, "God does it for others, but will He do it for me?"

About thirty five years ago, I was just starting out in the ministry God had for me to do. I was the Music Minister of a church in a small town with services three times a week (some people would drive 45 minutes just to come to church).

I opened the church doors around 5 am on weekdays. About 10 or 20 people would stop by to pray (as long as they wanted to, usually about 15 or 30 minutes), and then drive on to their work in the big city nearby. Then I would lock up the church at about 8 am, and start my day painting.

My roommate, Dave (who rented a room in my three bedroom house) did not own more than a duffle bag worth of items along with his guitar. He would hitch hike everywhere. He played his guitar while I played the piano for church.

One day he asked me if his friend John could stay with us for free, sleeping on the couch. (I had 3 couches at the time). I said it was fine for the time being.

John was diabetic (type I). I knew nothing about diabetes at that time. Dave gave John insulin shots three times daily as needed. John's wife, Betty, was a nurse's aide, and was not able to care for John because of her hectic schedule. She lived in a one bedroom run-down house on the other side of town.

I was dating my present wife at that time. A few months later, I announced to Dave that I would be getting married, and that he would have to find another place to live. He took the news very well, saying that he could see it coming.

Now moving forward... My wife and I have been married 30 years. We have lived through good and bad times. At the present, our house was foreclosed, and we needed a place to live. I did have a job. Another friend of mine offered use of a small trailer in his back yard. We were barely making it financially.

One day, I met Betty in a nearby Wal-Mart. John had died, she had re-married, and was now a nurse. She wanted me to meet her at a certain location the next day. I did, and she handed me a Wal-Mart bag with a roll of toilet paper, saying that she wanted to bless me for all that I had done for her in the past. (The toilet paper was just in case someone was watching).

I went home, opened the bag, and there was an envelope inside with $5000 cash. Timing could not have been better.

God does take care of us. We need to trust Him and rely on His Word and He multiplies what we give.

PERSISTENCE
by Barbara J. White

> Also [Jesus] told them a parable to the effect that they ought always to pray and not to turn coward (faint, lose heart, and give up)...However, when the Son of Man comes, will He find [persistence in] faith on the earth? – Luke 18:1, 8 AMP

I remember as a little girl I could be quite persistent! I had a mind set that insisted on my own way. I pleaded my case with my father after asking for something I wanted, saying, "but I need it!" My emphasis being on the word "need." I am so thankful that my parents corrected and trained me and I learned to submit to their authority. My parents did not break my spirit but disciplined me as they should. But as an adult I have learned the value of being a persistent believer.

Persistence is not wrong if it is used in the right context. *Persistence* means: to continue steadfastly or firmly in some state, purpose or course, especially in spite of opposition.

I learned from the Word of God that persistence is a godly spiritual force that will enable the believer to endure in spite of opposition or discouragement. It is a spiritual tenacity to be added to our life of faith and prayer. Peter mentions this in 2 Peter 1:6 where the Holy Spirit tells us to add spiritual ingredients to our faith. For example, to self-control we are to add steadfastness (patience, endurance) Amp. Bible.

We need to exercise persistence in order to obtain the promises of the Lord and resist every attack of discouragement from the enemy. Satan has come to do three things – *steal, kill and destroy* and he must be resisted by the believer. Through God's grace He has helped me to operate in a godly persistence that has brought amazing results in my life and ministry.

Don't give up so easily when you know the will of God for your life. His will is revealed in His Word. When symptoms of sickness hang around don't give up, keep on believing the Word of God and obtain your provision of healing. When grief and depression try to hold you in bondage, and the devil says you will never get over it, persist with the Word of God on your lips. God has provided life and wholeness after loss and disappointments.

Our Heavenly Father is not upset with His children when they insist on having what He has provided for them in Jesus. We aren't being disrespectful when we ask in faith and receive our needs and godly desires. It gives God great delight when His children obtain everything He has provided for them. Be childlike in believing God's Word and taking hold of the promises! Father God takes pleasure in our prosperity for spirit, soul, body and, yes, financial needs too! You "need" everything He has provided for you in order to live an abundant, overcoming life of victory! (Psalm 35:27)

THE BLESSINGS OF OUR HEALER
by Karen Y. Ranney

Sharing with others God's miracles and healings is what delights my heart. I would like to tell you about some healings in my own life. God delights to bless His children.

For almost 37 years I had anxiety and panic attacks. I was miserable, but yet still praised God. I was prayed for and believed Jesus Christ was my Healer. It had been such a long journey of many torturous days and years; to the point, I could hardly drive without an attack of anxiety and panic. I loved Jesus, went to church and praised God many times when I did not feel like it. Actually, I wondered if I would live that way the rest of my life—BUT GOD!

He is able, Faithful and true! I had prayed many times for God to deliver me from this oppression. Through it, I did learn to cry out to my Lord and Savior Jesus when I had an anxiety/panic attack…and they would subside. BUT PRAISE GOD! After meeting my husband, who is a praying man, God showed me His great love for me though my husband, and I was healed completely of the anxiety/panic attacks. It feels wonderful to drive all I want and be in crowds with no anxiety. Hallelujah!

About the same time, after meeting my husband, we would pray together over the phone before bed. I had dealt with insomnia for about 37 years also. I wondered if I would ever be able to fall asleep easily. BUT GOD, [again] was so good to me and I started falling asleep while my, now husband, would pray with me on the phone at bedtime. It was funny! I would wake up with the dial tone on the phone in my ear. God is so good! What a wonderful heavenly Father we have!

I am thrilled to also testify that God has wonderfully blessed me with a healing after 22 years of living with a neck and back injury as a result of a car accident. I have paid thousands of dollars for chiropractor, physical therapy, MRI's and orthopedic medicine. I have had numbness and nerve pain that would rob me of sleep every night. My husband prayed for healing for me every night since we have been married. Needless to say, I was getting very weary.

I prayed earnestly one day, *"God, I don't understand. I know You can heal me. I have waited longer than the woman with the issue of blood, who had it 12 years. Will You please heal me for Your glory?"* In fact, I had asked my husband a couple of weeks prior to this, *"What do you think about me getting laparoscopic surgery?"* He said I could, but I never felt God's peace. He seemed to be telling me to wait.

A short time later, the numbness started going away and the pain all over my upper body was gone. Wow! I was healed after 22 years.

THE GIFT OF THE ANOINTING
by Jeane Batty

In the age we are living, people do things in such ordinary ways, even disrespectful ways, it shows no reverence for divine purpose.

One of the most beautiful words in the English language to me is—A*nointing*. What does it mean? *Anoint* means to bless somebody with oil. To rub oil or ointment on a part of someone's body, usually the head or feet, as part of a religious ceremony, for healing or consecration to sacred duty. It also means to ordain or to install somebody officially or ceremonially in a position or office.

Anointed One, is a noun and means one chosen by divine election. *Jesus is The Anointed One.* Throughout the Bible this word was used when anointing kings, people of God, the Tabernacle, or objects set apart for sacred use.

Acts 10:38 we read "And you know that God anointed Jesus of Nazareth with the Holy Spirit and with power. Then Jesus went around doing good and healing ALL who were oppressed by the devil, for God was with him." 1 John 2:27 NKJV But the anointing which you have received from Him abides in you, and you do not need that anyone teach you; but as the same anointing teaches you concerning all things, and is true, and is not a lie, and just as it has taught you, you will abide in Him." We have the anointing of the Holy Spirit living inside of our spirit. His attributes, His gifts, His power, His enablement. What an awesome gift Jesus has given us through His anointing.

There are different types of anointing. There are at least seven and possibly more: preaching, teaching, praise and worship, healing, prophetic, deliverance and prosperity. We need to learn to respect and protect the anointing within us. We should always follow His lead and walk in the anointing He chooses for us.

There is a sweetness about the anointing. Our lives require the anointing in order to be effective in the Kingdom. It can do more in a second than we can striving in the natural in a lifetime. The anointing destroys the yoke of bondage and sets captives free, brings healing, restores relationships and brings provision. God has equipped us for service.

> Ephesians 2:6 AMP
> "And He raised us up together with Him and made us sit down together giving us joint seating with Him in the heavenly sphere (by virtue of our being) in Christ Jesus the Messiah, the Anointed One."

A VISION—GOD'S HEALING RIVER
by Aaron Jones

While pastoring a small church in Oklahoma, I remember one Sunday night, I was sitting on the front row as a guest Evangelist was preaching. Suddenly, I sensed something moving from left to right just above my head. I looked up into a river of human body parts flowing 3 to 4 feet wide and maybe 3 feet deep, with the bottom just over my head.

Immediately the Spirit said, *"Healing always comes. These are extra new limbs, arteries, nerves and organs continually being supplied for the Body of Christ. My Church is to be healthy—HEALING ALWAYS COMES!"*

I thought: what about Sister____, she died with cancer? Or Brother _____, he left early? Why wasn't he healed?

God's Spirit replied, *"Healing always comes. I did not say, it is always received."* Many miss the healing flow, because they are not looking (stedfast gazing; expecting) up (for) to receive from Heaven. People have problems, people down here have sickness and issues. God up there, has all the answers, healings and miracles. But they will never by faith reach up into that heavenly river of supply and take possession of what they need, as long as they are focused on earthly things. It's as if God is calling us to venture out into His pure waters of provision for every healing or miracle needed, but we are standing on the shore crying for Him to help.

Since that vision, every time I feel symptoms of any kind coming on, I get my hands up. I want them up praising God, up reaching for His promises, up reaching into that river of supply.

> Revelation 22:1 KJV
> And he shewed me a pure river of water of life, clear as crystal, proceeding out of the throne of God and of the Lamb.

The river of God's provision is flowing, expect it, reach for it! It is yours by faith—TAKE IT!

∼

I CAN'T STOP
by William Paul Howard

I can't stop believing
That when you took those stripes
For my healing
I was healed.

I can't stop believing
That when you died on the cross
For my sins
I was forgivin

I cant stop believing
That on the 3rd day
You rose again
To prove that we win

You defeated the devil
And walked on this earth again
Then you gave the dead a chance
To be forgiven of their sins

You now have the keys
Of Death, Hell and the Grave
That we could in our life
Walk in victory and be brave

I can't stop believing
Passing from this life to the next
I'll be with you
Finally at rest

GOD KEEPS CONFIRMING HIS WORD
by Steve Farmer

For verily I say unto you, That whosoever shall say unto this mountain, Be thou removed, and be thou cast into the sea; and shall not doubt in his heart, but shall believe that those things which he saith shall come to pass; he shall have whatsoever he saith."
— Mark 11:23 KJV

God just keeps confirming His Word in me... for a few years, I had an unusual mole that had come up on my forehead. In the last few months it had grown quite large and was turning colors and several had remarked that I better get it looked at. Finally, I had to go meet a new doctor with our new insurance at work, and he said he was really concerned about it and wanted me to make an appointment to get it looked at.

As I was at the church building praying, I picked up the anointing oil and anointed it and said in the Name of Jesus.... the next morning, before Sunday's service, I looked in the mirror, and it was gone!!!!!

His Word is still being confirmed daily!!

A BRAND NEW HEART
by Jim Andrews

Jeremiah 32:27
Behold, I am the God of all flesh. Is there anything to hard for me?

I was prompted by the Holy Spirit to call a friend. I called and was told that her sister neaded a new heart and there was nothing the doctors could do. She was in heart failure and was given a death sentence unless she received a new heart.

The GOD of the MOUNTAIN III

I prayed for the sister over the phone. I was given a *word of knowledge* and said: the doctors will say, *"I don't understand her heart is pink like a baby's heart?"* Confirmation that it was the Lord that had given her a new heart. The doctor checked her the next day and ran tests: the results came back and the doctors confirmed what was spoken by the Holy Spirit. He didn't understand it, but her heart that [was] in failure was [now] 'pink' like a baby's. God had given her a new heart! This was a sign to her that she truly had received a new heart. She was discharged in two days.

> Ezekiel 36:26 KJV
> A new heart also will I give you, and a new spirit will I put within you: and I will take away the stony heart out of your flesh, and I will give you an heart of flesh.

He not only gives us a new heart spiritually, but He gave her a new heart physically as well. What was impossible with men, was possible with God. To God be all the glory!

> Psalm 107:20 KJV
> He sent his word, and healed them, and delivered them from their destructions.

GOD IS YOUR ANSWER; NOT YOUR PROBLEM

by Bruce A. Higgins

The next major point you need to know about God is this: God isn't your problem.

Many people go through life thinking and believing that God is mad at them or that God doesn't ever want them to have anything in life. But the Word of God doesn't say that. In fact, it says the opposite:

> Beloved, I pray that you may prosper in nevery way and [that your body] may keep well, even as [I know] your soul keeps well and prospers.
> — 3 John 1:2 AMP

God wants to bless and prosper your life. You're not living a blessed, happy life when you're sick, broke and defeated. I know because at one time in my life, that's exactly where I was. I was sick in my body, lonely in my heart, and defeated in many areas of my life. But the Lord changed all that when I started reading His Word and believing what He said, instead of what I thought or what I had been incorrectly taught. I learned that it was the devil who wanted me sick and defeated in my life, not God.

Before that, I was like someone from another country visiting the United States for the first time. That person doesn't know what U.S. law says, so he believes what he is told, even if what he is told is wrong.

That's how it has often been with our perception of God. We've been told some things that aren't true about Him. For instance, many of us have been taught that God brings sickness, lack, or trials into our lives to teach us something. But that isn't what Jesus said in John 10:10:

> The thief comes only in order to steal and kill and destroy. I came that they may have and enjoy life, and have it in abundance (to the full, till it overflows).
> — John 10:10 AMP

The above verse tells us that it's the devil who comes into our lives to steal, kill, and to destroy. But Jesus came that we might have life more abundantly!

Notice that the Bible says Jesus came so you could enjoy life. But if you live your life your way, you will never really know God's peace and joy in your heart. If you give your life to Him, you will have true peace and joy. God wants you to enjoy life, and He wants your life to be pleasing to Him.

BLESSINGS AND SUCCESS
by Daryl P Holloman

1. BLESSED (HAPPY, fortunate, prosperous, and enviable) is the man who walks and lives not in the counsel of the ungodly [following their advice, their plans and purposes], nor stands [submissive and inactive] in the path where sinners walk, nor sits down [to relax and rest] where the scornful [and the mockers] gather.
2. But his delight and desire are in the law of the Lord, and on His law (the precepts, the instructions, the teachings of God) he habitually meditates (ponders and studies) by day and by night.
3. And he shall be like a tree firmly planted [and tended] by the streams of water, ready to bring forth its fruit in its season; its leaf also shall not fade or wither; and everything he does shall prosper [and come to maturity].
— Psalm 1:1-3 AMPC

People who follow the advice of the ungodly, people who follow the plans of the ungodly and people who follow the purposes of the ungodly are guaranteed to be cursed, unhappy, unfortunate, unprosperous or unsuccessful and unenviable or undesirable.

Walking and living in the counsel of the ungodly produces the aforementioned negative results or fruit simply by refusing to do what the Bible says to be Blessed, Happy, Fortunate, Prosperous and Enviable.

Such refusal can be either known or unknown to the person rejecting the Bible principles.

Christians who love Jesus and serve Jesus cut themselves off from the Blessings of God and the Prosperity promised in His Word, merely by paying more attention to integrating in their daily lifestyle the things they see and hear on television, movies, the internet, news reports and any information or opinions they may be exposed to on a daily basis in their own home, the homes of friends, at work, at school, at the mall, at the grocery store, at the post office or even at Church or anywhere else they may be exposed to the words and opinions of other people.

Even the music they listen to or sports events they watch or listen to can expose them to the advice, plans and purposes of the ungodly; especially if said Christian does not spend very much time *searching the Scriptures* and *meditating upon the Word of God*, spending personal time to think upon the things that are written in the Bible and how to apply the Truth of Scriptures in their daily lives, as a filter to produce the Blessings and Success they seek in prayer.

Standing in submission with sinners, inactive in speaking and doing the Scriptures, plus sitting down and relaxing with people who scorn and mock the principles of the Bible, will block a Believer from the Fullness of Heavenly Blessings.

The Spirit of Truth is the Spirit of the Word of God [meditate upon John 17:17] and the more a person gets in agreement with the Spirit of Truth and the principles of the Word of God, then the more the Bible Blessings and Prosperity will manifest in the life of the Believer.

FROM EMPTINESS TO A FLAME
by Darla Faye Beattie

God has taught me how to love, have hope, and have faith. Through all my sin and being lost, He never gave up on me. He taught me to love myself.

I wandered aimlessly, feeling lost, empty, hopeless, and unloved. For years, I sought to fill the void inside me. I tried drinking, smoking, lying, cheating, and endlessly seeking the approval of men to try and feel whole. I got into relationships with men who abused me, and it became so normal that I never realized they were hurting me. I didn't think I deserved better, because it was all I knew. When I hit rock bottom, something inside of me told me to go to church. I began speaking to the Pastor, and suddenly, the emptiness inside me transformed into a flame, and that spark grew to ignite my whole life. I changed the way I lived, learned how to love, and realized my duty to love myself and share God's love with others, just as He used His Church to help me understand what it means to feel whole. In all of those years I spent searching, God never abandoned me. He was waiting for me to come home. God gave me His love, grace, and salvation. He was the missing piece, and it was He Who gave me peace.

God is my strong tower. He taught me that I am worthy of love as the daughter of the most High King. Greater is He in me, than He that is in the world. He is my hope, salvation, and my destination.

WILL YOU PAY THE PRICE?
by Brian Ohse

The Lord spoke to me in 1 Kings 5, saying: **"It cost to build a foundation."** But it may be more than you are willing to pay. However, if you have these foundational stones, you have a powerful promise. Look at 2 Peter 1:8

> "For if these things be in you and abound, they make you that ye shall neither be barren nor unfruitful in the knowledge of our Lord Jesus Christ."

But what are the "things" that must be in us? First, *"faith,"* for without it, there's no pleasing God. (cf. He 11:6) Then *"temperance,"* which is a continuation of self-restraint, meaning: you're not running your mouth, instead you are allowing the Holy Spirit to speak. So be quick to listen and the Holy Spirit will give you the right words. Thirdly, *"patience,"* something we all need to work on. I think of the Scripture,

> "Let patience have her perfect work, that you may be perfect and entire, wanting nothing."

Then I got a real eye-opener, when I looked up patience in Webster's, for not only are we to walk in *the highest of excellence* in character, we're to be *delightful* people in all aspects. But too many of God's people are walking around broken, bruised, beaten and bloody. Why? They've forgotten how to use His Word as a weapon. I think of the Scripture, "The weapons of our warfare are not carnal, but mighty through God to the pulling down of strongholds." Then the Spirit impressed me to look up *"entire"* in Webster's: it had many truths hidden in seven definitions.

First, *"Having no part missing,"* every area of your life He's involved in. From your prayer time, to ministering to others, He's always in the center of things. Second, *"unbroken,"* meaning: Circumstances have not unraveled you. You're standing steadfast, even through the tears—you refuse to change *your confession of faith*. Third, *"unmixed,"* meaning: your spirit and your flesh no longer operate together. Even as Paul said, *"It's no longer I that lives, but Christ that lives in me."* Then fourthly, *"pure,"* as I think of the verse, *"Create in me a pure heart and renew a right spirit within me."* But what was David really saying through his prayer? His cry was, *"Put something there that wasn't, and put back something that once was."* So ask Him to return you to your first love. So all these stones must be evident and operating in our lives. For if they are, we'll never be barren or unfruitful. Meaning, the gentleness and kindness will always be there. Then most important, you will always be pregnant with the Word—ready to give out life to those that need it. So cry out for the *"things"* to be made full inside you, and you will reach a hurt and dying world with His life.

THE THREE CROSSES
by Bobby Lampkin

In Matthew 27:37, they nailed the sign above Jesus' head that read, "This is Jesus the King of the Jews." There were also two other criminals that were being crucified with Jesus. Also, the chief priests, the scribes and the elders were mocking Him. Saying that He can't even save Himself. What they didn't realize is that Jesus was dying on a cross for everybody. At the crucifixion site there were two other criminals who were also nailed to crosses, Luke 23:39. Jesus was paying a price that criminals would pay, even though Jesus was not a criminal, but to the Jews He was not the King they expected.

Three in Scripture means excellence. What does *excellence* mean? It means that it doesn't have to be done again. Jesus was in the middle of the other two guys that were nailed to the cross. One on the right and the other on the left side. The criminal on the left sounds a lot like the flesh. Save yourself and us. This criminal was also mocking Jesus and saying what the other Pharisees were saying. The criminal on the right said, this man has done nothing wrong, but yet He is being crucified like we are. The criminal on the right said, remember me when You come into Your Kingdom. The criminal on the right is symbolic of the cry of Adam. There was no price for sin back when Adam sinned in the garden. Now we see the criminal asking Jesus to remember me. To *remember* means to put back together like it was; [Re-Member] — or put my members back together. Make me right with God again. This criminal repented and confessed his sins to Jesus and realized he made a mistake that led him to where he was. The criminal on the right side was in *self-denial* when he didn't fall into the trap of everyone mocking Jesus. It's easy to the flesh to do the things of the flesh, but it's harder to follow after what the Spirit is saying. Jesus then tells this criminal you will be with me in paradise. He will be forgiven and made right again.

So, there are three things I want to leave with you today. One, have a repenting heart towards God. God isn't mad at you and you shouldn't be mad at yourself, shake off that thing and get back up because you are better than how you are feeling. Second, always have a heart of thanksgiving. Be thankful that Jesus' blood cleanses us from all unrighteousness. Jesus' blood is what makes us right with God again. Three, have self-denial. You may have to tell yourself no sometimes. When you wake up in the morning, say, self you are not going to have a bad day today. Self I am not going to have a bad attitude today. Do you want peace in your life today? Then peace comes with honor. Where there is no honor, there is no peace.

FIRST KNOWING THE GIFTS OF THE HOLY SPIRIT
by Ron Kelley

Years ago when coming into the knowledge of *operating in the gifts* of the Holy Spirit, I attended a church service with my friend Karl, an Evangelist from Chicago. (I had met Karl at a revival in Sand Springs, Oklahoma.)

I had just received *the baptism of the Holy Ghost* a short time before and had no idea what was going to happen next. I was struggling with the *speaking in tongues* in public; although, speaking in private was okay.

We went to an Assembly of God Church out west [I think in Perry, OK]. After the service we were visiting with the Pastor and others who were lingering, when one of the people asked the Pastor for prayer about a desire he had in his heart. I heard him say, *"my daughter has been gone (a run away) for several weeks,"* and this father was asking for her safe return. It was then that I heard a Voice in my spirit; no one else heard. I had never experienced this before; yet, I knew it was God, I just didn't know what to do about it. It was partly that I was afraid to say anything and partly not knowing how to say what I was told. i didn't say anything until Karl leaned over and whispered: *"What did God just tell you?"* I told him and he said, *"You have to tell this father what God said to you.*

The Holy Spirit gave you the Word and you have to give it."

We walked over to the father of this missing child and Karl said I had something to tell him. This is what I heard, **"Go home your daughter is on the front porch waiting for you to get home."** The father hurried home.

I was told via the Pastor and Karl that she was actually where God said she would be. The father told Karl to be sure and let me know she was there just exactly as the Word said she was. That was the first "Word of Knowledge" I had received and the Holy Spirit became more alive ot me from that time on.

Thank you Jesus!

THE STORY OF LITTLE JAKEY
by Rachel Allen

The first day of school seemed to be like any other. There was a buzz of excitement in the air for a new beginning. Most felt this, but not everyone.

The driveway was backed up with vehicles unloading children and it wasn't hard to tell which were well cared for considering their new clothes and shiny shoes.

Suddenly, a loud, rusty car caught my eye. I always endeavored to encourage the underdog with words to affirm them and identify internal strengths. That car was my mission.

His name was Jakey. Jakey didn't get out of the car, so a teacher opened the door with a smile to greet him. Jakey crossed his arms, growled and kicked at her. It was his first day of kindergarten.

Jakey's parents had been neglectful, maybe not purposefully, but it had stunted him physically, emotionally, socially and academically. Every day he came to school in the same urine-smelling clothes, so the school nurse gave him different clothes while she washed his. Still each day he came back filthy. He didn't know A-B-Cs, 1-2-3s or to follow Principal Losaka's directions and he stole food from classmate's plates. As an educational team, we started looking at Maslow's hierarchy of needs to help him adjust to school life. Our principal, Mrs. Losaka instructed us to love Little Jakey even more when he was naughty.

Little Jakey was swiftly placed in foster care and his neighborhood school changed, so we said "Good-bye, we'll miss you."

More than a year later I'm living in a new state and come across a photo of Mrs. Losaka on facebook. I smile as it warmed my heart remembering how much she loved the children in her school. In the ceremonial picture were 2 other men and a child and I suddenly realized I knew one of the men. It was Judge Davidson whose juvenile courts I had worked in many years ago, several years before I knew Mrs. Losaka. I was confused, but suddenly, I realized Mrs. Losaka was in the photo with Judge Davidson and Mr. Losaka—and the child was little Jakey! The Losakas had adopted him! I was stunned, amazed and elated!

Then I heard the Lord say, *"I did that for you."* He meant I'm adopted as God's child, cleansed of my past, given a new home, a new family, a new name and declared an heir of God.

> Romans 8:14-17
> "For as many as are led by the Spirit of God, these are the sons of God. For you did not receive the spirit of bondage again to fear, but you received the Spirit of adoption by whom we cry out, "Abba Father." The Spirit Himself bears witness with our spirit that we are the children of God, and if children, then heirs – heirs of God and joint heirs with Christ."

THE BATTLE
by Aaron Jones

The problem tries to dominate your thoughts;
so, you go to The Bible in search of relief.
Fear tries to keep you from doing what you ought.
Then you rise up in faith and declare your belief.

This huge dark mountain looms in the distance,

The GOD of the MOUNTAIN III

The attack comes with lies, symptoms and pain,
You know it's Satan's last stronghold of resistance.
By speaking God's Word you can level this plane.

When you boldly resist him, the devil has to flee.
Though symptoms worsen as you speak to the pain.
Just stand on The Word and by faith you will see,
Your healing come quickly, and a great victory you'll gain.

Reading, "by Whose stripes you were healed,"
Then Psalm 91, Matthew 8, John 10 and Mark 11:23,
Though weak in body, your faith starts to build.
"I rebuke this sickness, I'LL HAVE NO DISEASE!"

The hours of battle turn into days and then weeks,
You pray, study, speak and dare to believe,
You're not shaken or stopped as you continue to speak.
Keep calling for the answer, you've already received.

The devil turns up the heat in the final moments of battle,
sending people to mock you and spew out negative talk,
with reasons for failure, thinking your faith they can rattle.
You cinch up your armor and continue to walk.

Faith, comes by hearing and The Promise you've heard,
"Mountain get out of my life and be cast in the sea!"
Your miracle is here—BECAUSE YOU SPOKE HIS WORD.
Rejoice child of God, for YOU ARE HEALED...
AND TOTALLY FREE!

SOLD OUT TO GOD'S MISSION
by Ginny Bridges

Missionaries aren't always seen in foreign language classes on their way overseas. Missionaries aren't always seen in pulpits speaking of their callings as they garner support. Missionaries aren't always seen teaching about Jesus in nations around the world.

Missionaries are simply people who are sold out to the call of God on their lives, no matter what it is or where it takes them. So if you go to an office, stay home with your children, stand behind a cash register, get your hands dirty under the hood of a car, tend the animals on a farm, teach social studies to middle schoolers, play Taps in a cemetery over the weeping family of a veteran, hold a stethoscope to a baby's or grandpa's chest, or whatever you do, if it's God's plan for you and you do it for His glory … then you're a missionary. Someone on a mission. God's mission.

THE SPIRIT OF JEZEBEL
by Michael Nokes

I had never heard of *the spirit of Jezebel* until a few years ago. When I did, a series of remarkable events were occurring. I had two good Pastor friends teach me about this spirit shortly after meeting a woman. They had no prior knowledge of her or our introduction. Unknown to me, she was operating under its influence. *God's timing is perfect.* He gives us what we need, when we need it. For me, this was spiritual verification! When this spirit attempted, God had already raised His Standard in my favor. It was a bumpy ride, but He prepared me just as he always does.

I learned the Jezebel spirit manipulates and/or attempts to dominate and attack, especially male authority. Its ultimate goal is to disable Christian leaders that possess the gifts of prophecy and/or of discernment.

Both Jezebel in Kings of the Old Testament and Revelation in the New Testament operated under the cover of religion. Its religious deeds are done for all to see. People under Jezebel's *influence* are often trying to make up a love deficit. They oftentimes have deep wounds from past rejections, fears, self-preservation, and the *root of bitterness.*

People influenced or controlled by the spirit of Jezebel use flattery to entice you. Jezebel spirits are masters of manipulation, utilizing guilt and undermining or discrediting another's influence. The Jezebel spirit attempts to seek out people of influence to gain their ear, win credibility, and get them to do their dirty work. Only an Ahab lets a Jezebel spirit operate unchallenged. This spirit often discourages a spiritual leader from his appointed place by character assassination and/or ruining his reputation. Those under Jezebel's influence can cause their children to grow up insecure, disrespect their fathers by forcing sides, and to become distrustful toward God's true authority.

In John 10:10 (KJV), we see that the thief only comes when there is *something to steal*. We see in 1 Kings 21:25 that Jezebel encouraged, enticed, and provided passion to Ahab's wickedness. And in Revelation 2:20-23 we see that Jezebel considered herself a religious person, but only served Satan to seduce the true servants of God away.

We rebuke this spirit because it destroys God's true image of love and trust in the family structure and defies His order in the Church. We secure the future for the Body of Christ as Elijah did in hopes of breathing life into dry places. God's love offers redemption to those under the *generational curse* of Jezebel. It can be broken, order can be restored, and the Spirit of God can be poured out turning the hearts of the fathers back to the children.

HERE'S A SIMPLE PRAYER: Father forgive me, I trust You and obediently submit to You. I rebuke the works of wickedness and rebellion. I will honor delegated authority in my life, by Your help. Thank You for a new beginning of holiness, purity, and humility based on Your Word. Amen.

GOD IS GOOD
by Renee Dowling Brophy

Years ago, I went through a tough trial that only the Holy Spirit could get me through.

My husband and I had been in a New Age commune and separated when he turned cruel. God reached me, and told me to go to my father's in Nevada. There I got born-again by God's great mercy.

After 1½ years and being filled with the Holy Spirit, God sent me back to Massachusetts to my husband in the New Age to get him saved. It was an assignment, as I had to deal with *witches* and *warlocks* that wanted him in the occult, and also deceived friends, to get him out.

When he finally came around to want to leave, he still had to be saved. We moved into a deep woods with a couple he knew in New Hampshire. It was in the winter, deep with snow. They had one loft over their garage, and we had a tent. But, we managed it all.

None of them were born again. All were in great bondage from New Age, drugs, and liquor. The woman was a difficult challenge to overcome. Because of incest since very young, she had a lust problem with many men, and was attracted to my husband. She also had four abortions, and didn't realize it was a baby until the fourth one. She walked around half naked as her lifestyle, and so the men called her "earth woman." My husband had been a Marine in Vietnam, and also had a deep lust problem.

One evening after I knew she was going after my husband I went out into our car and wept before the Lord. My Father in Heaven kindly spoke to me: *"Do you see all those many stars?"* It was a cold, yet beautiful, night and the sky was filled with stars. *"Yes." "For every one of those stars there is someone that is lonely."* He filled me with His peace and let me know that was her real problem.

Jesus said, *"In this world you will have tribulation, but be of good cheer, for I have overcome the world,"* from John 16:33. God gave me love, faith, and perseverance to help win these three to salvation.

One trial at a time. He kept me from one year to the next. Eventually, the Lord got them all. They got saved and filled with the Holy Spirit. It took a long time with the sensual lusts involved, but God got the victory.

That couple went on and got married, and had four children of their own. They felt God gave them just the little children that they wanted. Her husband thanked me for letting God use me for his family. God got that victory over the flesh. Then, they went on to Bible school for ministry.

My husband finally got it all right with the Lord, and he's gone on to Glory now.

And, for me? I learned God—IS GOD. One day at a time. Bless the Lord oh my soul!

STAND UP TO THE DEVIL!
by Bruce A. Higgins

You see, there is a devil in this world who hates you because you were made in the image of God. The devil wants to destroy your life. But if you will learn who you are in Christ and then *act in faith* on that knowledge, you will stop the devil in his attacks against you and continually experience God's peace and victory.

1 Peter 5:8-9 tells you what you have to do in order to overcome the devil:

> Be sober [alert], be vigilant [watchful]; because your adversary [enemy] the devil, as a roaring lion. walketh about, seeking whom he may devour: whom [or you] RESIST STEDFAST IN THE FAITH.

This Scripture reminds me of a boy who went to my Junior High School in California. This boy's name was Butch, and he had a reputation for being a real bully. Butch always had a gang who followed him around. Everyone knew not to mess with him because of his reputation.

One day, a new kd named Bob enrolled at our school. Shortly thereafter, he had a run-in with Butch. Bob accidently bumped into Butch one morning walking through a crowded doorway. Butch got mad and challenged Bob to a fight after school.

To Butch's amazement, Bob accepted. At the end of the school day, there was Bob waiting for Butch. Everyone had thought Bob would chicken out. But Bob was new to the school and he didn't know all the stories of how tough Butch was. When Butch realized Bob wasn't afraid of him, that bully tried to talk his way out of the fight!

That's how the devil is. As long as you believe the stories and lies he tells, he will stop you in life. But as soon as you start telling him what the Word of God says—as soon as you stand up to him and let him know you're not afraid of him, he will try to talk his way out of the situation by telling you the Word is not true.

Jesus said in John 8:44 that the devil is *the father of all lies*. If you don't guard your mind with God's Word, Satan will try to speak to your mind and lie to you. That's why 1 Peter 1:13 warns you to brace up your mind and stay alert.

Always remember—SATAN IS A LIAR!

THE CURE FOR FRETTING
by Barbara J. White

Fret not yourself because of evildoers, neither be envious against the workers of inequity... fret not thyself because of him who prospereth in his way... fret not thyself in any wise to do evil...
– Psalm 37:1, 7-8

Did you notice three times David exhorts us by the Holy Spirit to "fret not"? It would be well for us to find the antidote for *fretting*. What is the Bible cure?

The word *"fret"* in Hebrew means: worry, be anxious, dread, fear, be concerned, be angry, be irate. Thank God we have a Bible cure for fretting! Let's look at the Word of God.

DELIGHT YOURSELF IN THE LORD. Let Him be your joy, your song and your strength (Psalm 28:7-8, 37:4).

COMMIT YOUR WAY TO THE LORD AND BE CONFIDENT. You cannot commit someone else's way to the Lord but you can commit your way by doing verse 5. *Roll and repose each care of your load on Him.* (Psalm 37:5 AMP).

BE STILL and REST IN THE LORD. Faith is not only a good fight but it is a rest for the spirit and the emotions (Hebrews 4:3, 9).

BE PATIENT – WITH YOURSELF AND OTHERS. Let the force of patience undergird your faith. Ephesians 4:2 AMP says: *we are to bear with one another and make allowances because we love each other.* "To stand" (to exercise patience) is not the apex of faith (believing). The first admonition is to "DO ALL" (Ephesians 6:13) – do all the Word has instructed you to do; that includes FRET NOT!

> Casting the whole of your care [all our anxieties, all your worries, all your concerns, once and for all] on Him, for He cares for you affectionately and cares about you watchfully.   – 1 Peter 5:7 AMP

WHY SACKCLOTH AND ASHES?
by Ed Marr

The following excerpt was taken from
"FREEDOM IV — *Armed and Extremely Dangerous*"
▪ Used by Permission.

Matthew 11:20 – 22
"...they would have repented long ago, in sackcloth and ashes..."

Why sackcloth and ashes? *Sackcloth* was worn as a symbol of mourning or penitence, often with *ashes* sprinkled on the head. Sackcloth was made of black goat's hair, which was a very course fiber and is very similar to the texture of burlap or wool. Natural resources such as jute, hemp, twine and the like were not readily available for the desert traveler. However, there were plenty of goats! The desert travelers entwined the goat's hair together on a warp (weaving machine) to make blankets of woolen sackcloth and other garments known as woof. *(cf. Lev. 13:48 – 49)* The *ashes* were obtained from the cooled residue of a fire known as a sin offering. Scripture teaches that the penitent either *sat, laid or wallowed* [flop about, squirm] in ashes. Ashes were also placed on the head, the face or beneath the one making penitence. This practice was a way of acknowledging to God, the *carnality* lodged within the soul of the penitent and the penitent's desire to suppress his carnality as indicated by those ashes beneath the penitent. *(cf. 2 Sam. 13:19; 1 Kg. 20:38; Est. 4:3: Job 2:8)*

> TRUTH: **Whereas, water submersion represents the death, burial and resurrection of Jesus Christ and the saint's identification to these, likewise, the wallowing in ashes represents the saint's recumbent position in the water unto repentance. Upon his surfacing, the saint becomes born of that meta-water!**

This understanding gives the expression, "holy roller" a fresh new perspective, doesn't it? *(cf. Mt. 3:11; Jn. 3:5; Rom. 6:1 – 6)*

Just as water baptism is an outward display of the spiritual *new birth* from within, likewise, sackcloth was used as an outward display of penitence, which reflected the condition and the contrition of the heart, as that affliction of the soul. That condition being, iniquitous thoughts, evil imaginations and all ungodly fancies.

> <u>Truth:</u> The blood of Jesus Christ identifies the love of God, who is first Love, for His love covers a multitude of sins. Similarly, the sackcloth portrayed that covering of God's expressed love towards the penitent. What's more, the sackcloth also represented the overlay of the sacrificial blood of the sin offering as well as the saint abiding in his first love! *(cf. Rev. 2:4 – 5)*

After all, God did not require that the animal's blood be smeared or applied to the person's own body, but the Priest was required to throw *the blood* round about and against the altar. *(cf. Lev. 3:2, 8)* In like fashion, the sackcloth was a blanket that was thrown over and round about the penitent!

WHO IS THIS JESUS?
by Wayne Sanders

I was at the archway in St. Louis on the Fourth of July several years ago. Two young girls came up to me kissing and touching one another. They began to attack me say Jesus is just a fairytale written in a book called the Bible.

I was kind of surprise by their aggrressiveness towards

me, because I never said or did anything to attract their attention. I did comment back that I thought it was very conveinent that they would be of that oppinion considering they were using it to justify what they were doing.

They had the right to their own oppinion, but one day they will look back on this encounter and realize they had an opportunity to meet Jesus, Who raises people from the dead, which I have never heard of a fairytale doing that before.

So, there are people that believe Jesus is just a good story or a fairytale. Pastor Louie Giglio made these statements that deserve our attention. "Was he truly who He claimed to be in the Bible? Was He truly God or just a good teacher? Is He King of kings as He claimed to be? Or was He just a pawn in the power struggles of His time? Is He the only way to God or is He just another of many that people claim as a path to eternal life? Is He the all powerful Lion of Judah or the sacrificial Lamb of God for humanities sins?" (See: Mathew 16: 13-16 NKJV).

Father I pray, that together we can experience your goodness, mercy, love, and your grace. And that you are also leading us to understand your sovereignty, divinity, wisdom, and power. In Jesus name! Amen!

                Blessing on the journey.

THE SHEEP ANSWER
by Roger K. Lane III

Mike Pope, Rod McLain and I were asked to speak in Wisconsin before and during Resurrection Sunday. The Church provided a place to stay; a bed and breakfast on a farm. Very nice. The owner was also a Pastor at another Church. He had a big barn on his land next to the bed and breakfast. He invited Mike and I to join him in the barn. Inside were several sheep in a large corral. They were spread out doing their own thing in several places. Some were munching on hay, some were laying down, others were just leaning on the rails.

"Y'all want to see something cool?," the Pastor asked us. We said *"sure."* He started saying *"Here shepa, shepa, here shepa, shepa."* Suddenly the sheep started baaing, looked in his direction and they all came to where he was. He said hi to them and petted a couple and then little by little they all went right back where they were before. He asked Mike to try the same thing. Mike started shouting what the Pastor had, but not one sheep baaed. Not one sheep looked. Not one sheep came. The Pastor asked me to try. I thought, I bet I can get them to do something. Same, same as Mike, nothing. Then the Pastor called out as before. Every one of them came running. [An eye-opening experience.]

True sheep know their Master's voice
—and the sheep answer.

THE AARONIC BLESSING
by Allen Ranney

The Aaronic blessing is one of my favorite passages in the Bible.

> Numbers 6:22 – 27
> "And the Lord spoke to Moses, saying: "Speak to Aaron and his sons, saying, "This is the way you shall bless the children of Israel. Say to them:
>> "The Lord bless you and keep you;
>> The Lord make His face shine upon you,
>> And be gracious to you;
>> The Lord lift up His countenance upon you,
>> And give you peace."
>
> "So they shall put My name on the children of Israel, and I will bless them."

Think about what this passage entails. We understand what it means to be blessed, or do we really? To be blessed of God is to experience full favor from the Creator of the heavens and Earth. The Hebrew word for blessed is (*Barak* #1288). The primary meaning is *to kneel,* that doesn't make a lot of sense to a 21st century Western Christian mind set. To really understand it we must think about it from a 1st century Judeo-Christian mindset, a Kingdom mindset.

In antiquity, to have an audience with the king would be a great honor, you would enter the court of his presence and he would either extend his scepter towards you or not. To enter the king's presence without his express permission was certain death. But if you were extended the scepter, you could come before him and kneel. You would bring your petition before him and he would consider it. During this time of consideration, the king might have only glanced at you, may even have been scowling in irritation. In the ancient world you ran the risk of punishment by making the king angry. Then if the king was pleased, he would grant your petition usually by *lifting up his countenance* towards you, *making his face to shine* towards you. In other words the king would smile and show his pleasure to you. What a great honor it would be to have favor in the king's sight.

As repentant, born again, Christians we have been granted this grace by the King of kings and Lord of lords, Yeshua Messiah/Jesus Christ Amen. We have been made priests and kings by Him (Revelation 1:6) and can come into His presence anytime without fear, as the middle wall of separation has been removed (Matthew 27:51). We have been blessed with His peace, His *shalom*, which is an everlasting peace in His presence. Rejoice the King smiles on us.

A CALM MIND AND HEART
by Rachel V. Jeffries

Proverbs 14:30 says in the Amplified Bible "A calm and undisturbed mind and heart are the life and health of the body, but envy, jealousy, and wrath are like rottenness of the bones."

In verse 29 it says if we are slow in anger, we have great understanding, but he who is hasty of spirit, exposes and exalts his folly.

STAY IN FOCUS

We are not of the world even though we are in it. Therefore, we fight with God's Word to stay in focus with Him and not be part of envy, jealousy, and wrath. If you have ever been the brunt of a jealous, envious and wrathful person, it is not fun. *Jealousy* leads to anger and rage. Actions usually follow. This is where we get road rage and other murderous things happening today.

ONE SIGN OF GRIEVING

One of the signs of grieving can be *anger*. You are angry at the person for leaving you. You may be angry because they did not take care of themselves. There are many reasons to be angry. If they left you in a lurch financially, spiritually and emotionally it can surface with anger. So undealt with anger, jealousy, or envy can lead to wrath and actions unbecoming to us. One of the big keys is to *recognize* it, ask for forgiveness. Even though the person is gone we *forgive* them. Also, we need to get our mind on HIM Who will never fail us. He provides in the midst of trouble; He gives us new life and more abundantly. Sometimes you must just say, *"I let it go."* Look in the mirror and say, *"I let it go."*

We serve a God of peace and order. So, let Him do the ministry in us today.

PRAYER: Holy Spirit, You are life, peace and order. I yield to Your personality and ask that You flow through me. Anger, jealousy, rage and wrath you have nothing to do with me. Forgive me Lord, wash me clean of any of these works of the enemy. I choose to listen to You Lord and not make my life and other's lives miserable by yielding to the flesh. Fill me today with all that You are in Jesus' Name. AMEN!

CONFESSION: I am holy as He is holy. I confess He has made me brand new through Christ. I am a new creation serving God with all my heart, mind and spirit. He is the greater One living in me. I choose today to walk in the goodness of God and not the deceiving thoughts of Satan. My heart is clean before the Lord. I confess His knowledge flows through me. I confess it, possess it and walk in it through His power today. HALLELUJAH!

ADOPTION
by Lynn Whitlock Jones

I once heard an adoption case in court. The judge asked the biological parent this question. *"Do you understand that if I terminate your rights, in the eyes of the law, you are dead to this child?"*

Because of Adam's sin of rebellion, we are born as children of sin and under the rule of Satan. Galatians 3:26 declares that we are all sons of God through faith in Christ.

Therefore, when we are born again we are adopted as Sons (and daughters) of God.

As I was thinking about this, the Holy Spirit began to show me that as adopted sons of God, we acknowledge the fact that our "biological parent" is dead to us. And we must realize that the devil is no longer our father.

In Galatians 2:20 Paul declares that he has been crucified with Christ and it is no longer he that lives, but Christ who lives in him. This applies to all believers.

Galatians 4:4-5 states that we receive the adoption as sons and that the Spirit of His Son cries out "Abba Father". This enables us to have the relationship of Father and son established in our hearts. It is also becomes a legally reality.

An adopted child has to learn to call their parents mom and dad. A new believer has to learn to call God, Abba Father. Just as an adopted child can choose to look for and find their biological parents, we can choose to go back to the devil and his rule. However, God still waits for us to come back to Him.

We must understand and walk out the truth of this statement: *"In the eyes of the law, Satan is dead to us!"* He legally has no right to us anymore. Once we recognize that he has no right to us, we can truly walk in the position of a son and the authority of that position!

STEREOTYPES
by Ginny Bridges

Do you ever notice that the world is full of stereotypes? Here are a few: Hollywood portrays all southerners as ignorant bigots. They show all nurses as buxom nymphomaniacs. Some would have us believe that every long-haired, tattooed man is a druggie or that every energetic, creative child has ADHD. And isn't it true that every Texan wears boots and a cowboy hat?

I've also noticed there are misconceptions about God among church-goers. Some see Him as an angry judge Who keeps score of all our misdeeds and Who is eager to zap us when we step outside His tight box of rules and regulations. Others envision God as a benevolent genie Who will bestow on them any whim as long as they recite perfectly memorized prayers of petition. Then there are those who perceive that He is so generous with grace that they are guaranteed a life free of consequences for any decision or act.

Not one of the above statements is true.

∼

CLEAN OR UNCLEAN
CALLED-OUT OR THE SAME
by Adrienne Gottlieb

1 Peter 2:9
"But you are a chosen race, a royal priesthood, a holy nation, a people for God's own possession, that you may proclaim the excellencies of Him who has called you out of darkness into His marvelous light;"

Are we different from the world? If we are indeed called-out, shouldn't we be different? When the world looks at us, ought it not see something special? Why are our divorce, abortion, and illness statistics the same as the world's? Why do greed and hypocrisy seem to be the labels the world uses the most against us? What is wrong?

Mark 7:6-9, 13 KJV
6 (Jesus) said unto them, Well hath Esaias prophesied of you hypocrites, as it is written, This people

honoureth me with their lips, but their heart is far from me.
7 Howbeit in vain do they worship me, teaching for doctrines the commandments of men.
8 For laying aside the commandment of God, ye hold the tradition of men, [as] the washing of pots and cups: and many other such like things ye do.
9 And he said unto them, Full well ye reject the commandment of God, that ye may keep your own tradition. ...

13 Making the word of God of none effect through your tradition, which ye have delivered: and many such like things do ye.

Does this seem too harsh or ring of truth today? The Scripture distinguishes between clean and unclean citing which animals are acceptable to eat and which are not (Deuteronomy 17, Leviticus 11). Out of that arose all kinds of ritual concerning the utensils used to eat such animals. 2 sets of dishes, 2 sets of Passover dishes, how to bury the dishes if the milk dishes touched meat, etc, etc, etc. These were all man made regulations that became ritual and religious activities missing the meaning of the law; the separation of the clean from the unclean. We tend to do this often—miss the meaning and intent and develop ritual that makes us feel good. We blindly follow religious activities and traditions; simply because, it makes us feel good and we seem to want to blend in with the rest of the world.

Yet, we are to be called-out, separated from the world; yes living in it, but not of it. We are to be the head, give direction. Instead we follow. We make ourselves feel good with programs, with attendance, with throwing a little money toward the poor, with building edifices for our own aggrandizement, etc. I find it very troubling. No wonder we are ridiculed. The *hypocrisy* is stunning (at least in America). We have lost the sense of community and belonging because we are no different. We put God off in the future instead of *demonstrating* Him here and now.

Jesus summed it up in (v 13 above) "We've made the Word of God of none effect through (our blind following of religious activities--traditions). Simply because it makes us feel good.

It is my hope and prayer that the called-out people of God, The Church, will take its *rightful position* as the head and not the tail, as above and not beneath in every area of life on this earth.

A PRAYER OF THANKSGIVING
by Marcella Burnes

For God to be aware
The Saints of God are gonna ram it
Bombard and withstand it
The very heavens in God's hands
To overwhelm the commander at the helm

The GOD of the MOUNTAIN III

With the passionate plea
of the Saints that be
We're gonna paint the sky with love to Him on High
Make music to God's ear about the apple of God's eye
To tear down the walls till Jericho's do fall
Ram's horn adorn from the sheep he has shorn
Rebuke the thorn like Paul has worn
Until the cry rises to the sky
Of Israel's King let Messianic praises ring
Joy will roar as His Kingdom soars
Thankful we see as darkness flees

From San Francisco's halls till wisdom falls
The joy of the ages be stamped across the pages
Ancient ryhmes for modern times
Peter and Paul shadow standing tall
Merciful, merciful. I do hear, belief rising from each ear

Mountain moving, breaker proving, hospitality brooding
Anointing flowing, Spirit wind blowing
Hunger and thirst for righteousness first
A prayer of the ages be all the rages
A mighty wind flowing in
Gasping breath as we rest
For shook foundations of future generations
In closing I say prepare to be blown away
As Heaven's blessings flow to mere man below
Hallelujah to the King!
Let our breath this day ring!!!

DO YOU WANT A VISITATION
by Ginny Bridges

During a time of intercessory prayer before church service recently, I heard God ask, *"Do you want a visitation from the Lord tonight?"*

I immediately answered, *"Oh yes, Father, we do want a visitation from the Lord tonight."*

He queried again, *"Do you want a visitation from the Lord tonight?"* I found it strange to be asked a second time, but didn't hesitate to respond, *"Yes, Lord, we want a visitation from You tonight."* Let's be honest here. Who wouldn't want a visitation from God? Who would turn away or refuse such a gift?

His Voice came clearly again, *"Do you want a visitation from the Lord tonight?"* There was a few second's pause, and He continued, *"Or do you want Him to move in, to take up residence, to walk among the people in the fullness of His glory?"*

Immediately I fell before Him, repenting of my short-sightedness, and wept at the realization of what He was offering to our group of believers. Then I trembled at the prospect of His answer if I would dare to have the courage to ask what it would require of me to facilitate such a move of God—SURRENDER.

Complete and total surrender.
A Gethsemane experience.
Visitation or habitation.
Selah.

CONSIDERING HER FOR MINISTRY
by William Paul Howard

In the early Church, Men and women were not permitted to set together. Men and women think different, and *the men* needed their space away from *the women* to listen to the Priest and concentrate on God. Some early churches made the women set in the balcony, while the men set on the floor area.

Sometimes while the Rabbi was teaching and the women had a question about what was said they would call out to their husband disrupting the service.

> Women should remain silent in the churches. They are not allowed to speak, but must be in submission, as the law says. If they want to inquire about something, they should ask their own husbands at home; for it is disgraceful for a woman to speak in the church. — 1 Corinthians 14:34-35 NIV

Paul tried to correct this in a Letter to the Corinthians.

The biggest problem is that some *denominations* took this as a *thus saith the Lord* and made it a rule in the church, keeping women out of the ministry for years. Women could be Missionaries, but were considered servants more than actual Ministers of The Gospel. What doesn't make since is: that women were considered good Sunday School teachers, but was not considered for ministry.

Jesus saw that a woman could be an Evangelist in the woman at the well. She went and told everyone that would listen that she had met the messiah. Do you think that she would have been considered for ministry?

MAINTAINING A TEACHABLE SPIRIT
by Marty Clancy

2 Peter 3:18a
"But grow in the grace and knowledge of our Lord and Savior Jesus Christ,"

In order to grow as a believer, we must be teachable:

- We must <u>humble</u> ourselves in the sight of the Lord (James 4:10). A humble and contrite spirit says, *"Teach me, Lord, and help me."* As a result, He does, and we sense His abiding presence and know we are His habitation and home (1 John 3:24 AMP).

- We must watch what we <u>hear</u>. Mark 4:23-24 says "if any man has ears to hear, let him hear. And He was saying to them, 'Take care what you listen to.'" Hear what the Lord is saying. If we listen, we will grow and learn. In the gospels, when the multitude heard Jesus, they were healed and *set free*.

- The 3rd "h" is <u>heart</u>. Proverbs 4:23, "Keep your heart with all *diligence*, for out of it spring the issues of life." A right heart is pure and soft, giving and forgiving. Being quick to repent is the key. Our *reward* is being happy.

- Walk <u>holy</u> before God and man. Hebrews 12:14 says, "Pursue peace with all people, and holiness..." As we walk in the Light, our *conscience* is clear. The Holy Spirit, our Helper, gives us the power we need.

- Lastly, we must maintain <u>hunger</u> for the things of God, for all that He has for us. God has a banquet table served. He wants to fill us to overflowing. That is being truly blessed!

~

JESUS WAS A FRIEND
by Bruce A. Higgins

The woman at the well started talking religion:

Our fathers worshipped in this mountain; and ye say,

that in Jerusalem is the place where men ought to worship. — John 4:20

But Jesus was there to meet her real need; that being, to fill an emptiness deep inside her that religion could not. Jesus wanted to change her heart.

In John 4:6 it tells us that Jesus sat down at the well. He was touchable, and He was on a mission. Yes, He was tired, weary and hungry; but, He was there to touch someone else's life. Sometimes to be a real friend, means to listen to someone else's heart cry. Jesus did that, He listened to her heart's cry, and He saw her need.

> John 4:6 KJV
> Now Jacob's well was there. Jesus therefore, being wearied with [his] journey, sat thus on the well: [and] it was about the sixth hour.

Too many times we don't want to take the time to be a friend to someone. In my own life, when I was searching for help, God sent a man to talk to me about the things of God. He gave me a lot of his time. He wasn't in a hurry, he took his time and ministered God's love to me.

This man addressed many of my questions and took the time to show me God's answers from the Bible. He didn't rush me, he didn't pressure me, he just showed me God's love by his actions.

HEARTS FOCUS
by Lynn Whitlock Jones

In 1 Samuel 8 the elders of Israel came to Samuel and requested a king to be over them instead of Samuel (who was old) or his sons (who did not walk in his ways). They said *"Now make us a king to judge us like all the nations"* and again *"that we may be like all the nations."*

The children of Israel were called out of Egypt as a chosen special people, God's own to be separate and set apart as a holy nation. They forgot how God had miraculously delivered them from slavery and bondage, how He had provided for and taken care of them.

They began to compare themselves to all the nations and became dissatisfied with God's reign over them. Yet because they began to forsake God and did not serve Him, their comparison caused them to desire to be like the other nations. They began to covet what they did not have.

Dissatisfied with God, their desires pushed them to reject God and ask for a king. Even though the Lord told them through Samuel what the king would do to them, they ignored the *consequences* and demanded a king. So God gave them a king.

Comparison is a snare of the enemy that will cause a believer to become *discontented or dissatisfied* with God, His promises and His blessings. When we compare ourselves to others, we allow an envious or jealous spirit to rule in our hearts.

In James 4:2 (AMP), James warns of the behaviors of believers that result from comparison. "You are jealous and covet [what others have] and your lust goes unfulfilled; so you murder. You are envious and cannot obtain [the object of your envy]; so you fight and battle."

Jealousy, envy and *coveting* will cause you to kill the peace and joy from the Holy Spirit. It will cause a fight and battle within your heart and spirit between good and evil.

A person who is envious or jealous of other people and what they have does not realize who they are in Christ. By this, they are in effect telling God "that He is not enough". They are not confident in Him and His promises, nor are they content in Him or themselves.

> Proverbs 14:26a TPT
> "Confidence and strength flood the hearts of the lovers of God who live in awe of Him."

As a son or daughter of God, we have been given all things that pertain to life and godliness. This should give us *confidence* to be who God created us to be. This knowledge should cause us to reject thoughts and feelings of inadequacy and the need to compare ourselves to others.

We should not look at others seeking their blessings or their gifts, but be thankful for what God has given us. Proverbs 14:30 (TPT) says, "A tender, tranquil heart will make you healthy, but jealousy can make you sick." A calm and thankful heart is not focused on what others are doing or what they have, but is focused upon God and His goodness towards us.

Today I can choose to look in awe at God or I can choose to look at others and fall into the trap of comparison, dissatisfaction and reject God. I choose to have a tender and tranquil heart focused upon God.

THE INCORRUPTIBLE SEED
by Barbara J. White

I recently read an anointed article on healing which explained from the Word of God how healing is a harvest. It ministered to me and I want to share some thoughts along this line.

We all would love to have God's healing power bring us instant results, but that is not always the case. Sometimes *the gifts of healings* and *working of miracles* are flowing, and that is wonderful! Usually our healing is manifested as a harvest, based on believing the Word of God in our heart and releasing our faith with our words.

If we don't get an instant healing, called a *miracle*, we may think that God doesn't have other means to get your healing to you.

Our healing has already been provided and secured for us when Jesus paid the price with the stripes He bore before being nailed to the cross (Isaiah 53:4-5).

Since the Word of God is called the *incorruptible seed*, alive and full of God's power (1 Peter 1:23), we can access our healing through planting the seed of the Word into our spirit. Eventually the harvest of healing will come and manifest in our bodies, because the seed of the Word always produces after its own kind. Unbelief and words of doubt will stop the seed from producing, even though it has the capacity to bring for your harvest.

Every seed in *the natural realm* requires water and sunshine to grow and produce after its kind. When we spend time meditating on healing Scriptures, watering the Word with praise and worship, our harvest will eventually come. Time can be an enemy to keeping our eyes on Jesus, our Healer. So the sooner you forget about time and rest in God's Word and let His peace prevail over your heart, mind and emotions, the sooner you will see your harvest of healing come forth.

I exhort you to stand fast in your faith, undergirded with patience, praise and worship, with a joyful *expectation* that your harvest is coming forth. Healing belongs to you—purchased with the precious blood of Jesus. The unbreakable covenant of God's mercy and grace has made it available to the whosoever will believe and receive.

~

DOG WITH KIDNEY FAILURE—HEALED
by Jim Andrews

Psalm 138:8 KJV
The LORD will perfect that which concerneth me: thy mercy, O LORD, endureth for ever: forsake not the works of thine own hands.

We were asked by a friend to stay at their house and watch their pets while they went on vacation. we were told that their dog Fancie had *renal failure* and wasn't expected to live. She was hardly able to walk and wasn't eating much. The family loved their dog abd didn't want to put her on dialysis. We were praying that she would not die. Fancie could not even step up to get her food, so we brought it to her. I sat in the floor and prayed for her. Fancie went to the corner of the room and laid down by her food. The next day I saw one of the dogs running and jumping off a sofa. We were watching three dogs. I called to my wife and asked her if she saw Misty (the daughter) running and jumping around? My wife said, that's not Misty—that's Fancie, the dog you prayed for! She had been running and playing all day like a puppy. She was completely healed. When the family returned home from vacation, they were amazed Fancie was still alive. We told them she was prayed for. The dog that had kidney failure was healed and lived many more years.

FROM WHERE GOD STANDS
by Aaron Jones

Many Christians have a problem getting over their past mistakes and failures. They tend to look at their present condition and only see their past. Then when they look to the future (if they do), they limit that future to their current position and circumstances.

But God, doesn't figure our past into His plans for us. And as He looks at where we are now He only sees our bright future.

> Psalm 103:10 KJV
> He hath not dealt with us after our sins; nor rewarded us according to our iniquities.

> Jeremiah 29:11 NLT
> For I know the plans I have for you," says the LORD. "They are plans for good and not for disaster, to give you a future and a hope.

We must understand, mankind is standing in the present and looking toward the future and God. On the other hand, God is standing in eternity out beyond the future and looking back through our future at men in the present.

So look up Church, there is a new glorious day dawning... and God has already been there.

∽

HE SENT TWO ANGELS
by Susan E. Kirk

Hebrews 4:16
Let us then approach God's throne of grace with confidence, so that we may receive mercy and find grace to help us in our time of need.

The night continued. We were driving. We were following the map. It was pouring down rain. We finally arrived at a location that I recognized. Hallelujah! But we were not at the church. It was still another hour away. By this time, it was 10:30.

We continued driving to our destination. I was feeling better about the drive. But, to my surprise, it was not over, because we found ourselves on the side of the mountain looking down on Allende, our destination city. It had rained so much for so long that the roads were flooded and blocked. I had no idea how to get to our destination. What I did know is that we were not safe because it was almost midnight. Once again, I pulled over. I asked Shelly and Wayne to pray for a Star of Bethlehem to guide us through the blocked streets to our destination. They sat silent. I bowed and prayed.

We sat there for what seemed like an eternity when a vehicle passed us. I pulled out flashing my headlights. I was trying to get the vehicle to stop. I had no idea if the people were good or bad. The vehicle pulled over. Again, I gathered my notebook, pen, and dictionary. I walked up to the vehicle. I pointed to Allende. The man, in broken English, ask me what I needed. I broke down and cried. I told him and his wife that God had sent me a second set of angels. This time they spoke English. He smiled and said that he was Catholic.

I told them that we needed to get to the church in Allende. He asked me which church. I didn't know how to tell him so I asked him if he knew of the Catholic steps. Of course, he knew of the Catholic steps. He gave me directions which led me through the cemetery (only road not blocked). I thanked him and his wife. They drove on. I was trying to turn my vehicle around on the narrow mountain road when a vehicle was honking at me. I became frustrated and finally was able to pull over to allow them to pass.

Guess what, it was the couple who had just given me directions! The man said to follow him to the Catholic steps. WOW, my Star of Bethlehem. Praise the Lord!

The night is not over, tomorrow, Encounter III.

Again, focus on God's promises. God completes His promises. God answered my prayer according to Hebrews 4:16. This time, my Star of Bethlehem prayer was answered in the form of a Catholic couple.

Again, God *revealed* His promises to me that dark and rainy night in nowhere Mexico. Where and when has He revealed His promises to you? Remember them, all of them, and give God thanks daily for His promises.

TESTIMONY TO INSPIRE
by Ginny Bridges

Here's a testimony to inspire you and give you hope for your situation. I had a terrific need for a specific job to be done on my vehicle so I took it to the specialist to get an estimate. Well, let me tell you this ... specialists come at a premium price and while I trust God to supply my needs, something just didn't seem right about it. I'm not speculating that they padded the estimate (how would I know that anyway?). I'm simply saying that $1040 was more than I was willing to pay for that particular job to that vehicle at this time. They recommended that I try another business in town who might be able to repair instead of replace the broken part so off I headed. At first that fellow told me he didn't do that kind of job but was willing to look at it to see if he'd have another recommendation. I told him the other company had said he'd be my champion but he wasn't convinced of that himself. I quietly prayed while he investigated. After a few minutes, he went into his shop, got some tools, and came out to see if his plan would work. He tried with all his might to remedy the problem, but had no success until I (inspired by Holy Spirit as I prayed) suggested that perhaps I could hold the broken part down while he put in the fix. At this point I suppose he was willing to try anything, so I dug my hemostats from my lab jacket pocket and we went to work, side by side, perspiring in the heat of the day and chatting about various things. Voila! Success to the max! And guess what? He would not let me pay him. I repeatedly asked how much I owed him but he refused my money each time. Now that is more than a miracle, in my book. Not only did he save me $1040, but his willingness to help spoke volumes to me about the provision of God as He met my need through the kindness of this man. He asked only that I not reveal his identity.

The point of all this is that God cares about every detail of your life … your coming in, your going out, your highs, your lows, your temptations, your victories, your relationships, your finances, your health, your disappointments, your challenges, your progress … everything. He cares about everything. He sent me to find out the cost of what I needed then sent me someplace else to get what I needed at no charge … so I would know and understand that He meets ALL our needs. He could have easily provided the money for the replacement. But He chose instead to provide the repair at no charge. I don't understand why. I'm just thankful that He did. Trusting Him with this situation ... however He wanted to provide for me ... reinforces to me how deep, how wide, how high, how broad, and how fierce is His love for me. And YOU!

AWE
by Steven Conley

The world is full of many very beautiful things and places. I was born in a small town outside of St. Louis, Missouri and had never seen mountains until I went to Colorado. In the 70's the Air Force flew about 30 new recruits to Denver, and bedded us down in old barracks for the night. After waking up, I walked out of those old dilapidated barracks one [November] morning, and I couldn't believe there was such a thing as 'PURPLE MOUNTAINS'. I WAS IN AWE! I seemed to remember some words from a song... "for purple mountain majesties" ...something or another.

Later that year, I moved to California and saw the Pacific Ocean for the first time. I was in 'AWE' of an ocean. Later on I flew to London, England and was in 'AWE' of the British culture. It was even more fabulous than television. On my first occasion to fly to Asia the pilot announced that the flight would be 12 hours non-stop. Twelve hours in the air non-stop?! If it was taking us 12 hours to fly to the orient then how big was the earth, the sky, the oceans, and God? I was struck with an eerie and unusual feeling that I have come to understand is called—AWE.

The GOD of the MOUNTAIN III

Now it doesn't take much to impress a small town boy. But nothing or no one commands 'AWE' like Jesus. Psalms 65:8 says, They who dwell in the ends of the earth stand in awe of Your *signs*; You make the dawn and the sunset shout for joy. In fact He is so terribly 'AWEFUL' ….full of 'awe' that the Psalmist also writes…"Worship the Lord with reverence and rejoice with trembling. (Psalms 2:11)

Worship? That has almost become a sport in our church services, along with rejoicing, leaping, clapping, singing, but the trembling? The Lord wants us to *tremble* upon our beds and sin not?

Recently the Lord God opened a *dimension* of His Glory to me. The God of creation opened to my understanding that not only was I to rejoice, dance, shout, and clap! Not only was I to play skillfully on a string instrument and teach His Word, but I was to stand in 'AWE' of Him. Tremble, and do not sin; *Meditate* in your heart upon your bed, and be still. Selah. Psalms 4:4. Awe that brings stillness?

It means nothing to Him if our *reverence* doesn't produce awe. It's only exercise and heathen ritual at best without stillness, trembling, and great terror. Even upon our beds. After this encounter with Jesus I have been unable to sleep upon my bed in the same manner, as I trembled in both the day and night. I spoke aloud one night… *"I am in awe of you."*

One morning about 6:00 a.m. He made His arm bare. So now like the Psalmist, I can truly say,

"O' God, I stand in AWE!"

The GOD of the MOUNTAIN III

WITH YOU IN MIND
by William Paul Howard

With you in mind
He said He'd go
To the cross
So you could grow

Many times
He could have said no
Because of you
He had to go

The rugged cross
He had to bare
For me and you
Because He cared

He knew one day
Because of sin
It would be to much
We could not win

The load of all
The things we'd done
We needed Him
God's only Son

In Him we trust
He gave His all

For me and you
He loved us all

With you in mind
He said he'd go
To the cross
So you could grow

Believe on him
He's all you need
In Jesus Christ
You shall be free.

AN AWAKENING SONG
by Rachel V. Jeffries

The following song is included on this Author's CD
"AMAZING LOVE"

▪ Used by Permission.

So often when I wake up, I am singing a song inside. Today I woke up and it took a couple minutes, but a song rose up big. My spirit man is rejoicing with this song. I pray it touches you as well. It is a song the Lord gave to me about three years ago. As I grow and live in God, these songs He gives me really do come to pass in my life. Most of you have read my experience which was the topic of one of my writings. If you knew all the circumstances from where I came from you would know this song is absolutely a miracle. Somethings I still do not talk about just because it would edify the enemy. I always want to edify the Lord instead of giving the enemy any credit.

The words are:

> I AM FREE, FREE, FREE, YES, I AM FREE INDEED.
>
> I AM FREE, FREE, FREE, YES, I AM FREE INDEED.
>
> HE BROUGHT ME OUT OF BONDAGE INTO HIS MARVELOUS LIGHT I AM FREE, FREE, FREE, YES, I AM FREE INDEED.
>
> ON THE DAY OF PENTECOST IN THE UPPER ROOM THEY WERE FILLED WITH THE HOLY GHOST AND SPOKE WITH OTHER TONGUES.
>
> FOLKS WERE CONFOUNDED BECAUSE OF HOW THEY SOUNDED IN THE LANGUAGE OF THE SPIRIT THEY UNDERSTOOD.
>
> THEY WERE FREE, FREE, FREE. THEY WERE FREE INDEED. THEY WERE FREE, FREE, FREE; THEY WERE FREE INDEED.
>
> HE BROUGHT AN ANOINTING WHICH BROUGHT ABOUNDING LIGHT, THEY WERE FREE, FREE, FREE, THEY WERE FREE INDEED.

I know you don't know the tune. But I can almost guarantee you if you spoke these words out with gusto you would sense the power of God setting you free from every emotional trauma that has ever tried to affect your life.

I can see you walking in your kitchen your living room, bedroom and throughout the house shouting, I AM FREE. YES, I AM FREE INDEED.

∽

4 STEPS TO FORGIVING OTHERS
by Steve Young

Letting go of those harsh memories and deep hidden hurts in your heart toward the person who offended you or caused the pain is very difficult. Forgiving them can be even more difficult, however, in order to fulfill the commands from The Lord we must love and forgive so we too can be forgiven. Jesus said, *"But when you are praying, first forgive anyone you are holding a grudge against, so that your Father in heaven will forgive your sins, too."* (Mark 11:25 NLT) These are not my words nor yours, but those of Jesus Christ Himself. He also tells us, *"But I say, love your enemies! Pray for those who persecute you!"* (Matthew 5:44 NLT) and, *"By this all will know that you are My disciples, if you have love for one another."* (John 13:35 NLT) Paul also shared, "Get rid of all bitterness, rage, anger, harsh words, and slander, as well as all types of evil behavior. Instead, be kind to each other, tenderhearted, forgiving one another, just as God through Christ has forgiven you!" (Ephesians 4:31-32 NLT)

Here are some steps to help you stay in right standing with The Lord by forgiving others:

- Come to the realization that no one is perfect…including you. When the person who has caused the pain and anguish against us, we tend to automatically lose our perspective about them, and resentment and bitterness begin to settle in within our minds. Scripture says, "Not a single person on earth is always good and never sins." (Ecclesiastes 7:20 NLT) You, me, them – none of us are exempt.

- Never try to get even. This is the heart for forgiveness. Romans 12: 19 says, "Dear friends, never take revenge. Leave that to the righteous anger of God." If we take it upon ourselves to take revenge on someone, we have stolen the revenge from God. Think about that for a moment.

- Change your attitude with gratitude by adopting The Beatitudes. You've most likely heard the statement, "You are what you eat." I wish to expand that to, "The things that you think of, you will find that you will become." If you have thoughts of hate and resentment, you'll become a person full of bitterness versus if your thoughts are full of love, you'll become of person full of love, overlooking wrong doings, and willing to forgive. Do you want peace, mercy, love, and forgiveness in your life? Then memorize The Beatitudes that Jesus taught (Matthew 5: 3-10), adopt the attitude of gratitude, and become a forgiving person.

- Control your tongue. "A gentle answer deflects anger, but harsh words make tempters flare." (Proverbs 15:1 NLT) In the natural we tend to mimic other's emotions and comments, which is what the enemy wants us to do. Instead, speak with the leading from the Holy Spirit within you.

ANOINTED WORD FOR NOW IN THESE END TIMES
by Ron Kelley

I was recently in a powerful anointed service where a *message in tongues and interpretation* of tongues was given. The message related to the end times and the happenings of today's world events. After hearing again the recording I wrote the message.

Messages of the spoken Word are worthy to be written and remembered as the events unfold before our eyes.

What happened in the Book of Acts? The Christian faith was born. The Jews and the Gentiles were brought into the Kingdom of God. Pentecost, the Holy Ghost and gifts of the Spirit came into view for the Body of the Church. Jesus, the plan of salvation was being preached throughout the known world. Also the end of the age, the New Testament and the events of the Book of Revelation.

The quote:

"*For the Spirit is moving through the land. Eye has not*

seen, nor has it even entered into your imagination the thing I am preparing this minute. Things in the unseen realm, things in the seen realm, that your eyes are going to witness, the things that are recorded in the Book of Acts are but small, insignificant, minor, and minute compared to what you are going to see. For my Prophets have longed to live and see this day. This day, in which all things are going to come to pass: and you have been called to this time and this day for the very reason that I have put the anointing on you. I have given you a destiny, and your destiny is to live and operate in this day and be part of what I will do in you and through you."

By this it would seem to fulfill what the Bible says will happen in the end times. And we who are alive today get to see God's mighty plan unfold before our eyes.

[Word spoken in Holy Ghost tongues and with interpretation at Eagle Rock International in Broken Arrowe, Okahoma 2019]

ABOUT BEING LED
by Michael Nokes

Proverbs 3:5-6 (caps added)
"Trust in the LORD with all thine heart; and lean not unto thine own understanding. In all thy ways acknowledge him, and HE SHALL DIRECT THY PATHS."

As I learned to be led by the Spirit of God I discovered three basic steps in Mark 4:20, the Parable of the Seed and the Sower: Hearing, Seeing, and Doing (Walking it out and producing fruit).

Faith comes by hearing, and HEARING COMES BY THE WORD OF GOD. We must first receive the ability to hear or understand. This is unlocked or not, by God, based on our heart. Next, we must see or perceive in able to receive the engrafted Word into our hearts where it can abide. This process produces change or transformation. (Ananias laid his hands on Paul and simultaneously healed his physical and spiritual blindness.) Then the third step is obeying or following thru with the Word which leads us toward Holiness and Love. If we love God and our Neighbor, this should be natural for us to gravitate toward doing the compassionate work of Jesus.

Jesus said in John 10:27 that His sheep hear His Voice. And in John 10:8, Jesus said that all that came before Him are thieves and robbers, but that His sheep did not hear them.

I can still remember the year I spent meditating loosely on hearing and distinguishing the Voice of the Holy Spirit. I didn't try to rush it and it didn't come fast. However, toward the end of that year, I was headed home after training a client. I could see my house. Suddenly I heard His Voice just as plain as day. He said,

"Go get Michael a donut." I immediately obeyed without thinking. My heart had been prepared and made ready. The quickest route was straight ahead. However the Holy Spirit spoke again, *"Go the other way."* Again I obeyed without thinking; I turned the car around in the intersection. Right at the point of commitment, when my car was turned the other way, He spoke a third time. He said, *"I want to show you the work on the wall!"* I thought wow, wouldn't that be freaky if the wall work has started.

As I drove and thought, "What if!" I bubbled with excitement. In years prior, as the HOA Board President, we started a project of building a new border wall by the city street. And eight years later it still had not started. But this morning I was in for a surprise, a HOLY SPIRIT SURPRISE! My new route took me to the exact corner where the signs of the wall work had begun. A large piece of entrance wall had been placed on the corner and a footing had been visibly started. He cares about our cares!

> Psalm 37:23 KJV (caps added)
> "The STEPS of a good man are ORDERED by the Lord: and he delighteth in his WAY."

With wholehearted sincerity pray Psalm 139:23-24.

WHAT IS TRUTH?
by Bill Steinmetz

So, I must admit that I am a pro of procrastination. I have put off writing this short article for quite some time, a few months I should add. Sometimes it just does not feel right saying the truth, and that is a truth, but Jesus took it to the highest level when asked about TRUTH. Pilate said unto Him, Art thou a king then? Jesus answered, thou sayest that I am a king. To this end was I born, and for this cause came I into the world, that I should bear witness unto THE TRUTH. Everyone that is of the truth heareth My Voice. Pilate said to him this simple question, what is truth? Pilate recognized that there are many truths and sought to release Jesus to them knowing He was a just man. The Jews, when Pilate said he found no fault in Him, said we have a law, and by our law He ought to die, because He made Himself—THE SON OF GOD.

Pilate was, when he heard this saying, even more afraid; and went again into the judgment hall, and said to Jesus, who are You? Jesus didn't answer him. Pilate said to Him, You don't speak to me? Don't You know that I have the power to crucify You, and have the power to release You? Jesus response was simply this, you couldn't have any power against Me, except it were given to you from above: therefore, he that has delivered Me to you has the greater sin. From that point Pilate tried to release Him: but the Jews shouted out, saying, if you let Him go, you are not Caesar's friend: whoever makes himself a king goes against Caesar. At that point Pilate tried to release Him but we know the story, He was told they had no king but Caesar.

What I am saying is that as much as he wanted to, he couldn't release Jesus, the people didn't want it and Pilate was a people pleaser WHAT IS TRUTH? The TRUTH is, Jesus had to be crucified so that we could be redeemed from ALL of our sins, and the TRUTH is they are many.

Please read John 18 and 19 and notice that Pilate wanted to set Him free but for his survival's sake he let Him be crucified to please the people.

Father open our eyes that we might see You, in all that we may have to endure and the strength to withstand the darts of the enemy. Let us become more like You, with each new day—LET <u>THE TRUTH</u> PREVAIL.

TREES OF RELIGION
by Ed Marr

The following excerpt was taken from
"FREEDOM IV — *Armed and Extremely Dangerous*"
▪ Used by Permission.

Matthew 3:10
"And now the axe is laid unto the roots of the trees:..."

When you consider any fruit bearing tree, have you ever wondered to what purpose does the foliage serve? I certainly have. I was out walking along a tree line just recently and I asked the Lord to answer this very question. Immediately, my mind conceived this reply. *"The foliage of any tree protects and shields the fruit from the atmospheric elements, for without the leaves, the fruit would be damaged by them. Without the leaves, the ripening fruit could not grow into its full maturity."* So then, the foliage tents the growing fruit as though the fruit were in a green house, where humidity and temperature are properly regulated. When a fruited tree is in full bloom and its foliage is all dressed out for display, you could say that such a tree, is dressed out righteously. However, should a fruitless tree be in full foliage and have no fruit, then you could say that this fruitless tree, is not righteously dressed out. Apply this to a morally deprived churchgoer and the impenitent, and you could say that they possess a religious dress up only, but are thoroughly unrighteous in the eyes of God; because they lack fruit! *(cf. Ps 1:4 – 6)* Once again, we see the combined application and effects of heat and water within the greenhouse. This again denotes that faith and repentance go hand in hand and that they are to be monogamous, just as a man's spirit and soul are to be. *More precisely that the heat of faith and the water of repentance exist to bring a saint into a spiritual green house effect.* The result of which, is that his leaves shall not wither and the fruit he bears, shall be as a healing for all the saint comes in contact with! *(cf. Ps 1:1 – 3; Re 22:1 – 2)*

The GOD of the MOUNTAIN III

THIS IS WHAT YOU ARE
by Marcella Burnes

You're a weapon of war,
fashioned for sure.
For total annihilation
of situations,
Prepared from the flesh
to enter complete rest.

You're a bomb of aplomb,
Where wrong doing throngs
You're sent to right the wrong.

You're a wheel of appeal
For Heaven's real feel.

You're a champion of pause,
for the cause.

You're a testimony living,
a destination given.

You're a rare affair
of Heaven's air!

You're an effect,
to break the enemy's neck.

You're a dream
of real things.

The GOD of the MOUNTAIN III

You're a portion, releasing abortion
upon the contortion of God's Word.

You're a meal prepared to spill real nutrition
upon a mission.

You're a crossword puzzle
given to muzzle,
[the father of lies].
Every word created to intersect Heaven's eyes.

You're a harmony sung
to be flung ...across the skies!

You're a living testimony,
owning only future's dreams
Of things spoken,
yet unseen.

You're a wheel
within a wheel.
A cog to still the rise
of poisonous lies!

You're a favored son
of Adam's One,
Re-given his race to run.
A course adjusted from a busted trust.

I hear the dust clods falling
As the Spirit of God's calling
Shakes the realm of man's frame.

Out of the dust certain things must—arise!

You're a secret place,
of mysterious taste!
A shadow forewarned
of the Gospel being born.

You're an enigma of God's mind!

You're a feast
to release,
the realm
of his helm.

THIS IS WHAT YOU ARE!

∽

GOD IS A GOD OF ORDER
by Wayne Sanders

Psalms 19:1 KJV
"The heavens declare the glory of God and the firmament sheweth his handywork."

There is a God in Heaven, and yes, He has created all things. The man that says there is no god has been described so adequately in the book of Psalms 53. "Only fools say in their hearts there is no God, they are corrupt, and their actions are evil, not one of them does good."

Listen to this quote taken out of "The Miracle of the Scarlet Thread.:

"Not only do we know that God exists through His handywork; but, we also know of His existance through instict. We all have a built-in God-consciousness. No matter how far away we may be from God, we still know He is around. Our conscience, regardless of how hardened it may be. constantly reminds us that there is a God in Heaven Who created us in His image."

Religion has dictated to us that God is waiting to beat us down for even the smallest sin we commit. But the truth is: God says that He loves us and that it is His desire to bless us. He has written about it in His Word where He spelled out the conditions of *a covenant agreement* (promises) *signed and delivered through the blood* of His Son Jesus Christ (cf. Jer 9:23-24 RSV).

God is a God of order!

FINE TUNED TO HEAR GOD
by Lynn Whitlock Jones

On the way to church this morning, the radio was tuned to our favorite Christian radio station. As we traveled through an area, the station was fading in and out and other stations were bleeding over it. As soon as we got down the road a little way, it cleared up and played just fine.

We are like the radio in the car. We are to "receive" signals from God, which is His Voice speaking to us. And in turn we should broadcast to others what we've heard and learned.

Sometimes the world's noise and chaos can cause His Voice to fade in and out or it may even bleed over the sound of His Voice. We go along only hearing a part of what He has to say. Thankfully, God gives us opportunities to "fine tune" our hearing!

One way we fine tune our hearing is by being in church. You may ask, 'What does being in church have to do with our hearing God?' The Bible tells us that faith comes by hearing the Word of God. People speak words from God to us. We can hear Him on our own, but sometimes He has to speak through someone else to really get *our attention*.

Anointed men and women of God; the Pastors, teachers, worship team and leadership all prepare themselves to deliver God's Word and His message to the church body assembled together. They spend time in God's presence in order to clearly hear and speak what He has to say. They study and *stir up those gifts* that will teach us, encourage us and equip us. Shouldn't we want to be in church where we can hear what He has to say and be blessed by the anointing placed upon those who minister?

Hebrews 10:24-25 declares, "And let us consider one another in order to stir up love and good works,

not forsaking the assembling of ourselves together, as is

the manner of some, but exhorting one another, and so much the more as you see the Day approaching."

When we assemble together we consider one another, we stir up love and good works, and *exhort* one another. It is as we bond together, that we are able to be encouraged and stirred up. This will cause us to be fine tuned to hear God and then be able to share His Word, Love and Grace with others. If we aren't fine tuned we become garbled, in and out messengers who aren't able to bless others.

Operating in His gifts and anointing is only productive if we are fine tuned to HIM! It is my desire to be tuned in to the voice of God, receive His Word, and then be able to share that Word with others. I pray it is your desire too.

IS THE PROPHET AMOS RELEVANT TODAY?
by Adrienne Gottlieb

During the time of Amos, the Old Testament Prophet, the Israelites went to worship at Bethel, which means House of God. The problem? It wasn't God's house; God was in Jerusalem! At Bethel the higher echelon of the Northern Kingdom would burn incense and present their sacrifices at the altar. By the way, this is where Jeroboam, the first king of the North, set up golden calves. He felt he had to do such so that his people wouldn't defect to Jerusalem, or the South. Sounds like our churches today who are afraid their offerings will fall off if "their" people visit another church. Pastors have been known to say: "Better not go there, they teach lies, they are false prophets, they don't preach the Word" etc. So Jeroboam commissioned his own priests and instituted his own feasts. He told his people they could worship where they pleased and how they pleased, as long as they stayed in the North.

At this time Israel was prosperous (the Dow was over 26000) and politically secure, a time of successful military ventures. It was the golden era. Jeroboam II came to power and the entire kingdom believed that God was pleased with them; after all, they were prosperous. In the midst of this, the Prophet Amos appeared on the scene. His prophecy reads like today's newspaper.

God's people during this time were intensely and sincerely religious. Their faith degraded to culturally acceptable ritual. Worst of all, Israel's religious leaders sanctioned the political and economic status quo.

Amos opposed the powers of his day. With graphic details that make you wince, he describes how the rich crushed the poor, how sexual debauchery was prevalent, how the legal system was corrupt, how justice was sold to highest bidder, and how predatory leaders exploited the vulnerable. Worst of all, Amos told how the religious leaders aided and abetted all of this. To the Priests who defended, legitimized, and justified Jeroboam's political power, Amos delivered an uncompromising word of warning (Amos 7:7-17).

In the midst of prosperity, Amos predicted failure, war, and devastation. And the most startling of all, Amos said it was God Who would bring this upon the people. Amos' words spoke of moral failure in every level of society: the law, the leadership, the economic life, and even worship (church life) Amos saw luxurious living for the rich, exploitation of the poor, loose moral standards, corruption in public life and religious life. He saw a religious life based on ritual rather than piety.

For Amos, there was no "Mishpat" (justice) and no "Tzedakah" (righteousness or right standing with God). In the Hebrew, *Tzedakah* is an attitude which is needed to produce *Mishpat*. One needs right standing with God in order to be just. Because one is righteous, justice is done. Tzedakah is a condition of the heart. It is a relationship with God that allows justice to flow through you. Has anything changed today?

For Amos, Israel was God's chosen people, a covenant people; and should be held to a higher standard than other nations. What about us in America? We hold ourselves out to be a nation chosen by God and morally superior don't we? When justice (mishpat) is ignored, society suffers according to Amos. In fact, it dies.

THERE'S A BALANCE—MONEY
by Bruce A. Higgins

On the subject of money: we've all heard it said, "You can't outgive the Lord," which is true. But friend, you still need to pay your utility bills or you will be reading your Bible in the dark. In everything there's a balance.

THE DNA OF GOD IN US
by Ginny Bridges

Just a reminder for those who are getting pretty close to the end of their ropes. Keep in mind that Jesus didn't bring you this far to bring you just this far. Greater days are ahead. If we'll take our eyes off what's around us and in us, and focus on Him, His magnificent grace, His fierce love, His perfect plan, His merciful interventions in our lives, and His mighty hand of deliverance, then we'll be able to experience the fulness of Who He is.

On a side note, a while back, the Lord showed me that when I am tempted to slide back into the black hole of depression, I should check out my own thoughts and words. He revealed to me that the pull of depression on my life is equally in proportion to my spiritual laziness. I'm not talking about the "fake it until you make it" mentality. I'm speaking of *guarding* my heart from self-pity, *resisting* the devil, *overcoming* by the blood of the Lamb AND the word of my testimony, being on the *alert* for the fiery darts. He once put it to me this way (rather sternly, I might add) … *"I gave you your soul. Don't you dare let anyone else have control over it. That's what I mean by guarding your heart."*

We are born from above with the DNA of God in us. *We are more than conquerors.* Jesus in us is more than able to handle what's in front of us today. Hang in there!

GOD IS FOR YOU
by Michael R. Hicks

There are a multitude of people that do not know that God loves them. Many live a life full of misery, despair and trouble because they believe they just live and die with the life they were dealt. Many have been to a church, heard the Word of God preached and walked out in the same condition they were when they went in. It is a terrible thing when a person hears the Word of God and cannot comprehend it. They will come to the conclusion that there is no God or God hates them for the sins, the crime, and the offenses they have committed.

God is an awesome God and He loves us very much. He wants to take *care* of us, *nurture* us, and *fellowship* with us. This is one of the reasons He made us in His own image.

Jeremiah 29:11 NKJV
For I know the thoughts that I think toward you, says the Lord, thoughts of peace and not of evil, to give you a future and a hope.

God is not sitting in Heaven on His throne with a big stick ready to pounce on us when we make a mistake. He has extended more patience throughout the history of the earth than we can measure. His thoughts for us are peace and His peace is complete full of harmony, serenity and tranquility. Only God can give us this peace.

The world has a peace to offer also. But it is temporary, has problems and is full of consequences. If the world gives you peace, it will be sure to take it back. The nature of God and the nature of the world are complete opposites because deep down the world is antichrist and hates believers. The world will smile in your face, but behind that smile is a sinister scheme.

God is pure through and through. He designed our bodies, and breathed life into us and gave us the dominion over the earth. Even though mankind rebelled against Him, He still loves and does what we allow Him to help us. Meaning our obedience to Him. He sent Jesus to the earth to save us from our sins and to cleanse us from all unrighteousness. He took our sinful natures away and replaced His nature in our bodies. How awesome is that. And for those who believed in Jesus as the Son of God, He gave us the right to become sons and daughters of God.

God has given us a future with Him, Jesus, and the Holy Spirit now and later in Heaven. He has given us all the tools, which is Himself, to live a full and prosperous life in the Lord – proclaiming Him as our hope of glory.

So whenever the world comes to you with doom and gloom, remind them that you are sons and daughters of the Most High God, and you can also remind them of their future which is doom and gloom they tried to deceive you with and total separation from God.

NO NEGATIVES
by Aaron Jones

To "talk out of both sides of your mouth" is the act of saying different things about the same subject. Many Christians are doing the same thing with their Faith: They pray one way, e.g., for healing, a blessing, another's well-being, etc., but then negate that prayer *by saying*, or confessing the opposite?

EW Kenyon once said, *"One's faith will never rise above his or her confession."*

> James 3:10 KJV
> Out of the same mouth proceedeth blessing and cursing. My brethren, these things ought not so to be.

THINK ABOUT THAT! We don't want to pray for the blessing (the positive), but then confess the curse (the negative). Our confession should line-up with the Word of God; with what we are believing for.

We should call things like we want them, not necessarily like we see them. Things you are experiencing now are products (manifestations) of your past confession.

Jesus said, *"But those things which proceed out of the mouth come forth from the heart; and they defile the man."* (Mt 15:18)

I know several people, who are evidently believing the wrong things in their heart, because their confession is a non-stop barrage of negatives; this one is sick, oh we're not going to make it! I don't know what we're going to do? I'll probably get sick, or die early just like my daddy, etc. Ask one of these *Negativ'ites'* how's things going and [an hour later] you'll wish you hadn't asked!

In the Scriptures two powerful truths stand out about this subject.

- 1. God spoke the worlds in existence. Made in His image and likeness we can, like our Father speak our world into existence. What kind of world are you creating?

- 2. Samson killed a thousand Philistines with what

weapon?_____ I believe just as many lives are being destroyed each day with the same weapon.

Let's be a BOLD Word confessor, a builder, a creator, an asset to the Kingdom of God not a Negativite—always complaining and tearing down.

Pastor Mark Hankins preached a series "Hold Fast to Your Confession – Get a Grip on Your Lip"

...and King David said, *"Take control of what I say, O LORD, and guard my lips."* (Ps 141:3 NLT)

> Numbers 14:28 KJV (caps mine)
> Say unto them, As truly as I live, saith the LORD, AS YE HAVE SPO-KEN in mine ears, SO WILL I DO to you:
>
> Mark 11:23 KJV (caps mine)
> For verily I say unto you, That whosoever SHALL SAY UNTO this mountain, Be thou removed, and be thou cast into the sea; and shall not doubt in his heart, but shall believe that THOSE THINGS WHICH HE SAITH shall come to pass; HE SHALL HAVE WHATSOEVER HE SAITH.

(See also: Ro 10:10; Ja 3:2-5)

GOD DOES A WORK AROUND
by Roger K. Lane III

John Wesley believed, that God couldn't do anything on Earth unless asked by a human being. Kenneth Hagin talked about praying out the plan of God in tongues. Working with computers, sometimes, something doesn't work. You have to do it another way. We call it a work around.

God gave mankind authority on the earth. God holds Himself accountable to His Word and satan (small cap on purpose) is a legalist. God does a work around by praying through us in the Holy Spirit. God literally *calls those things that be not as though they were,* on our behalf. *He speaks things into existence* for us. I can pray, sure. God praying for me, through me? Well. . . (Romans 8:26)

I WANTA BE
by William Paul Howard

I wanta be I wanta be more like Jesus
I wanta be I wanta be more like Him
I wanta be I wanta be more like Jesus
Like the man Who knew no sin

When I walk down the street people will feel it.

They will feel the love flowing from Him
In Their mind they will see my Saviour
They will feel His love within

I wanta be I wanta be more like Jesus
I wanta be I Wanta be more like Him
I wanta be I wanta be more like Jesus
Like the man Who knew no sin

One day they will all know him
One day they will stand before his face
One day they will all know Him
And understand his Grace.

I wanta be I wanta be more like Jesus
I wanta be I Wanta be more like Him
I wanta be I wanta be more like Jesus
Like the man Who knew no sin.

THE FIRE OF THE HOLY SPIRIT
by Barbara J. White

When we were baptized in the Holy Spirit we were baptized with the power and fire of God (Matthew 3:11). Jeremiah described *the fire of God* as if there was a burning fire shut up in his bones. *"But his word was in my heart as a burning fire shut up in my bones."* (Jeremiah 20:9) The fiery Word of God got right into Jeremiah's heart and affected his bones. It sustained him during his times of discouragement. It motivated and fueled him to keep yielding to the power of God.

Like Jeremiah, we need more "fire in our bellies." Jesus said in John 7:28 that, ...*out of our belly shall flow rivers of living water.* This is a direct reference to the Baptism in the Holy Spirit. The term *fire* and *rivers of water* both refer to the power and anointing of the Holy Spirit. Unless the fire of God burns in the believer's heart, it certainly will not catch alight in the listener's heart.

Paul's Word to Timothy is God's Word to us today: *That is why I would remind you to stir up (rekindle the embers of, fan the flame of, and keep burning, the gracious gift of God, [the inner fire] that is in you ... (2 Timothy 1:6).*

The fire of God is IN YOU - the Holy Spirit is longing for you to *fan* the flame by *stirring* yourself up to pray in tongues often and be a mighty anointed vessel for His honor and glory.

The fire of God as a twofold purpose:

1. To expose the darkness and *burn* (consume) the works of the enemy.

2. To anoint believers - the Body of Christ - to flow in the dunamis power of the Holy Spirit, making us *flames* in the earth to *ignite* others. It *sparks* us to rise higher in the precious anointing of the Holy Spirit.

The GOD of the MOUNTAIN III

∽

THE LORD'S PRAYER
by Allen Ranney

Matthew 6:9-13
Our Father in Heaven,
Hallowed be Your name.
Your Kingdom come.
Your will be done
on Earth as it is in Heaven.
Give us this day our daily bread.
And forgive us our debts, as we forgive our debtors.
And do not lead us into temptation,
but deliver us from the evil one.
For Yours is the Kingdom and the power
and the glory forever. Amen.

When you make this prayer, that Jesus taught His disciples, your own, it becomes powerful to accomplish God's perfect will in your life. Simply rephrase and redirect a few of the key words. Example no longer pray "our Father" pray "my Father". See, we are children of God therefore we can cry out *"Abba"* Hebrew for father. Romans 8:16 reads, "The Spirit Himself bears witness with our spirit that we are children of God."

Abba אב - father is Strong's reference # 1, Nelson's Three in One reference #1 and the New American Standard Exhaustive Concordance reference #1.

I find it fascinating that the very first Hebrew word that you can look up in all these references is the word for *father*. When we embrace God as our Father first and foremost in our hearts and minds, all the love, grace, mercy and forgiveness He pours out on us makes extraordinary sense. Remember Psalm 103:13 reads, "As a Father pities His children, so the Lord pities those who fear Him. For He knows our frame; He remembers that we are dust". That's our Lord God in all His mercy.

Our Father's generous character shines forth in Psalm 50:10, "my Father" owns the cattle on 1000 hills" Amen. We can rest assured that when we pray, *"give us this day our daily bread,"* that our generous Father is ready, able and willing to send manna from Heaven. (Exodus 16:4)

When we pray, *"forgive us,"* our Father is just and willing to forgive and forget. (Psalm 103:3)

When we pray, *"deliver us from evil,"* our Father is our ready defense. (Romans 11:26)

When we pray, *"lead us not into temptation,"* our Father guides us into ways of peace and safety. (1 Corinthians 10:13) Amen.

It is amazing to realize we (believers) in Jesus/Yeshua have been included into God's family.

"Behold what manner of love the Father has bestowed

on us, that we should be called children of God! Therefore, the world does not know us, because it did not know Him. — 1 John 3:2

～

POWER OF GOD
VS. INTELLECTUAL CHRISTIANITY
by Marty Clancy

In 1 Corinthians 2:4-5, Paul says his preaching was in *demonstration* of the Spirit and power, and our faith should be in the power of God, not in the wisdom of men.

It is different, knowing God by *experience* rather than just in *theory*. The book of Acts is our example. God showed up and gave a great witness of Himself. If we have only "classroom" Christianity eventually some people become cynical and say this stuff isn't real. Real faith is alive! You can argue over words, but when God shows up in power—the arguments are over!

Two weeks before our granddaughter, Norah, was to be born, an ultrasound showed she had a significant heart defect. After praying and laying hands on our daughter-in-law for healing, a miracle happened. When she was born, Norah was immediately taken to the NICU. Examinations followed. By the 3rd day doctors could find nothing wrong. She is a healthy vibrant girl today!

One day I related Norah's miracle to an atheist friend of mine, as a witness to the power of God. He had no argument and said, *"I guess it's a miracle."* Intellectual Christianity says all kind of things God doesn't do any more. God hasn't changed. Jesus saves, delivers, heals, and gives us victory!

One Sunday morning I was battling mononucleosis and I was preaching that morning. Before I spoke, I went forward for prayer. As I took the mic to preach, every symptom left. The power of God prevailed. Hallelujah!

HE'S ALWAYS WITH US
by Ginny Bridges

Being outside one morning about 5 AM, I looked up at the dark sky and marveled at the beautiful moon and glistening stars. I pondered the Scripture from Psalm 19:1 ... "The heavens declare the glory of God and the firmament showeth His handiwork." Of course, we're all moved to appreciate His creation and beauty as we see a sunset or unusual cloud formation, or as we look at satellite photos of the very earth whereupon we live. But I began to wonder if there might be something more that the heavens would "declare." That led me to think about the moon itself and the one thing that came to mind is the timely rotation of the moon and the earth. What I realized is that the moon is there in the sky always. Always. It has been there since

God spoke it into existence, but there are times when it's not visible to our eyes. Its rotation takes it through seasons when it's obscured from sight. But it's there nonetheless.

That's when the heavens "declared" to me that it's that way with God too. He's always with us. He made *a promise* to us when He said He'd never leave us nor forsake us and He's never reneged on that promise. He's ALWAYS with us. But sometimes He's not visible to our eyes. Our circumstances can sometimes *obscure* our view of Him. Our fears can sometimes *conceal* Him from our awareness. Our prejudices can sometimes *hide* His face from us. But He's ALWAYS with us. Because He said so.

And as the moon *appears* to come and go, so it is with our *perception* of God. We assume He's against us because we're enduring hardships. We think He's not helping us based solely on the difficulty of the trial. We decide He's resisting us because of the lengthy duration of the hard times. The fact is that these *assumptions* are founded upon the viewpoint of each person. We *think*, because we can't see Him. We *decide*, because we don't hear Him. We *conclude*, because we aren't feeling Him. All our senses are compiled into these assumptions and conclusions.

But the TRUTH is that He said He'd never leave us. The TRUTH is that He said He'd overshadow us with His presence. The TRUTH is that He said He'd hold us in the palm of His hand ... whether we see, smell, touch, or hear Him at all.

As you meditate on this, understand that you get to choose

what to believe ... His Word or your feelings. His promises or your hearing. His truth or your emotions. His commitments or the circumstances around you. And from this perspective, it's very easy which to choose to believe—HIM.

LISTENING TO GOD
by Lynn Whitlock Jones

Today I had to pull a trailer hauling a golf cart for a customer of ours to a town close by. I am naturally cautious when pulling the trailer anyway, and especially when hauling other people's property. As I was coming up to an intersection in a little area where there are a few businesses, I thought to myself, 'I should slow down for the entrance to Dollar General and the intersection coming up'.

Just past the entrance, I began to really slow down because the guy behind me was riding my bumper and I didn't want him to hit me at the stop sign.

As I neared the intersection, a pickup turned the corner and as it did, the trailer it was pulling came loose and proceeded to travel right down my lane. As it was coming at me, I slowed to a stop.

It got within a few feet of me, veered slightly to my right and off into the driveway of the convenience store before coming to a stop. Whew! I don't believe the driver behind me was even aware of what was going on in front of me.

Before I pulled out of my driveway, I had *pled the blood of Jesus* over me, and declared no weapon of an accident, incident or breakdown formed against me would prosper. As I was telling Skip and my brother about how grateful I was that I had slowed down, Skip said *'And you were listening to the Voice of God and obeyed.'*

Was it the Holy Spirit speaking to me to slow down, or was it just me?

It occurred to me that I had listened to that still small Voice that cautioned me as I was driving. Because I was in tune to hear, I was kept from danger. God is still speaking to us every day and in many varied ways. His Voice is as the thunder, a still small Voice, a gentle nudge, an encouragement or warning from another believer, or His Written Word. If we will pay attention, we will hear Him and be saved.

AMBASSADORS FOR CHRIST
by Aaron Jones

Peter told the lame man at the gate, *"Look on us!"* (See: Ac 3:4)

Do you remember Jesus' prayer in John chapter 17?

> John 17:20-23 KJV
> 20 "Neither pray I for these alone, but for them also which shall believe on me through their word;
> 21 That they all may be one; as thou, Father, [art] in me, and I in thee, that they also may be one in us: that the world may believe that thou hast sent me.
> 22 And the glory which thou gavest me I have given them; that they may be one, even as we are one:
> 23 I in them, and thou in me, that they may be made perfect in one; and that the world may know that thou hast sent me, and hast loved them, as thou hast loved me."

Jesus had told the disciples, *"If you have seen Me, then you have seen The Father."* (See: Jo 14:9)

Therefore, we as believers (CHRIST'ians) ought to be able to say, *"If you have seen me, you have seen Jesus."*

When facing disease or lack, like Peter, with complete confidence (BOLDNESS) we can say, *"Look on us!"*

> 2 Corinthians 5:20 KJV (caps added)
> Now then WE ARE AMBASSADORS FOR CHRIST, as though God did beseech [you] by us: we pray [you] in Christ's stead, be ye reconciled to God.

Here is that same verse paraphrased:

> The conclusion is, now we are official representatives of the Anointed One, it's as if God is pleading with

you through us: we (believers) standing in Christ's position, pray for you to be made right with God.

You are on *assignment* (sent) from Heaven to *impact* this world with Heaven's Policies and Government, using God's Word, spreading Christ's Love, Authority and Power to every corner of the earth.

Rise up Ambassador for Christ and *fulfill your duties* as an emissary (representative) of Jesus Christ to this world. Share His love and speak His Word boldly, all of Heaven is backing you and your eternal reward is great.

> Mark 16:20 KJV (caps added)
> And they went forth, and preached every where, THE LORD WORKING WITH THEM, and confirming the word with signs following. Amen.

(See also: Mk 16:15-18; Lu 10:2-11, 16-20)

PULLING YOURSELF UP BY THE BOOTSTRAPS
by Rachel V. Jeffries

This is a thought that came to me this morning. Often life has a way of putting our physical bodies down, our minds depressed or a seeming of lack of support around us. It is during these times that we must do exactly what this old saying says. For you who do not understand this phrase, I researched the meaning.

This expression of pulling yourself up by your own bootstraps originated in the 1800s. It refers to the ability of a person to lift himself or herself up by bending over and pulling on the laces of their boots.

WHAT DOES PULL YOURSELF UP BY YOUR OWN BOOTSTRAPS MEAN?

If someone pulls themselves up by their bootstraps, they improve their situation by their own efforts. It seems it made an impression on their boss about their ability to take care of situations.

This old saying originating in the 1800's can be applied to us today. To me it means I am not helpless to get out of any situation which tries to hold me down. One morning I woke up with such a *heavy feeling*. I could hardly stand the *pressure*. My thoughts were stay in bed and get over it. My spirit said, **"Get moving and look at your goals for today."** I had the choice to yield to *depression* or to get moving as my spirit man was telling me to do. That means, I pulled myself up by the bootstraps and got moving in prayer for all the partners in this ministry, saying the Word of God over every circumstance and in a few minutes the heaviness was gone.

After fighting the Amalakites, David and his men returned to Ziklag to find that their wives and children had been taken captive by their enemies, and their homes burned. As a result of this tragedy, David's men turned against him. And David was greatly *distressed*; for the people spake of stoning him, because the soul of all the people was grieved, every man for his sons and for his daughters: but David *encouraged* himself in the LORD his God. (cf. 1 Sa 30:6)

(1 Samuel 30:6) Immediately after this, there was a radical change in David's men. Instead of stoning him, they followed him and overtook their enemies. They rescued their families and returned with animals and other plunder. Let's move toward our day with much effectiveness and vision. **Remember:** IF WE LOSE VISION, WE PERISH.

Blessings to you today.

THE GREATEST SCIENTIST TO EVER LIVE
by Michael Nokes

"Dedicated to Michael and Jacob, my beloved sons, who faced down fear and the fires of life to become Mighty Warriors for God"

I don't know how many years it took me to appreciate the verses below.....to really hear them in a very, very deep and meaningful way. In my flesh I could shed so many tears but in my spirit I am dancing with sheer amazement and wondrous joy. I love my sons and rejoice with them! They had their own fires to walk through and they were not burned. Jesus said that I and my children have been placed in his hand and no one on this earth and no one in the spirit can pluck us out because HIS FATHER placed us there. It was HIS WILL that placed us in Jesus' hand. I will forever PRAISE HIM!!!

We look up in the Valley! King David said: *"It is good for me that I have been afflicted; that I might learn thy statutes."* (Psalm 119:71 KJV)

> 1 Corinthians 1:27
> "But God hath chosen the foolish things of the world to confound the wise; and God hath chosen the weak things of the world to confound the things which are mighty;"

Have you ever pondered life questions such as: Why do bad things happen to good people? Or why does the bad person drive a nice car and live in a big house? Or why do bad things happen to the innocent and those with little strength?

Our flesh mourns and that is why it must come under subjection. *Chaos* is caused by sin, because everyone has "choice". These choices cause ripples like waves on a sea. It's not the storms and waves that deserve our attention; it is the Master of ALL.

There once was a man who pondered these things. Ecclesiastes 8:14, "...there be just men, unto whom it happeneth according to the work of the wicked; again, there be wicked men, to whom it happeneth according to the work of the righteous...". All Solomon's scientific research described in the Book of Ecclesiastes turned out to be vanity except one thing:

Ecclesiastes 12:13-14
"...Fear God, and keep his commandments..."
For God shall bring every work into judgment, with every secret thing, whether it be good, or whether it be evil."

Mighty Warriors read the Word of God and learn:

Malachi 3:3
"...he shall sit as a refiner and purifier of silver: and he shall purify the sons of Levi, and purge them as gold and silver, that they may offer unto the LORD an offering in righteousness."

Revelation 19:16
"...on his thigh a name written, KING OF KINGS..."

Revelation 1:6
"And hath made us kings and priests unto God and his Father..."

Ecclesiastes 8:4
"Where the word of a king is, there is power..."

Mathew 21:21
"...if ye shall say unto this mountain, Be thou removed, and be thou cast into the sea; it shall be done."

FOCUSED ON THE PRIZE
by Ginny Bridges

Last night sleep eluded me. After tossing a while, I arose and began to fellowship with God. I spent most of the time in prayer for our nation, our leaders, those with needs as Holy Spirit revealed them to me, and for our service people. So today I want you to be eagerly expecting your miracle. The Lord specifically spoke to me about those of you who have been holding on to His promises and who have been believing Him for a breakthrough. You might even be losing hope and are tempted to give up, to stop praying. You might be tempted to try to solve the situation by your own efforts or by the world's methods. But I'm here to tell you to stop with that. Remember that His arm is not too short that He can't reach down into the deepest pit (even ones you have dug for yourself) and rescue you and those for whom you have been praying. His ears are always open to the cry of His people and He's working even now to bring it to pass. Your season of pregnancy, of waiting, of preparation has not been unnoticed in the spiritual realm. Stay focused on the prize of the high calling and remain in faith with radical obedience because it's coming. It's coming. It's coming. The season of reaping is at hand. Rejoice and rejoice some more for your Deliverer is on the way with your answer. In Jesus' Name, Amen.

HE MUST GO THROUH SAMARIA
by Bruce A. Higgins

John 4:4-6 NIV
4 Now he had to go through Samaria.
5 So he came to a town in Samaria called Sychar, near the plot of ground Jacob had given to his son Joseph.
6 Jacob's well was there, and Jesus, tired as he was from the journey, sat down by the well. It was about noon.

The Word of God tells us that Jesus had a call from God (an inward witness, or Word from the Holy Spirit) telling Him to go through Samaria. The Amplified translates (v4) as: "It was necessary for Him to go through Samaria."

He had very little to do with the Samaritan people. [The Jews often avoided Samaria because of its hellenistic culture, worldly materialism, and its lack of concern for any spiritual progress.] But God sees the big picture; the end from the beginning.

WHY THE HOSTILITY?

Have you ever not liked someone or a group of people? We've all been guilty. *"I don't like those people"*; because, they took something from us; their skin color; attitude or politics, etc. We've all done it or at least thought it.

SOMETIMES HATRED SEEMS JUSTIFIED

There are times that it seems like our hatred or malice is somewhat justified. Because of past history with them, we feel we're right feeling the way we do about a situation.

The Jews answered and said to Him, *"Say we not well that thou art a Samaritan, and hast a devil?"* (John 8:48)

The Jews felt that hating the Samaritans was okay because of past history. They felt justified in their actions. They looked on the Samritans as dogs and outcasts.

The Jews so disliked the Samaritans, they would travel miles out of their way in a hot and hostile enviroment to avoid them. That's what hate will do to you—it'll cost you dearly.

The Jews believed the Samaritans had taken their land during the Babylonian captivity. Matters grew worse when the Samaritans built their own temple and declared Mount Gerizin was the true place of worship.

The situation was ripe for a schism between those in Samaria and the orthodox Jews whose capital was Jerusalem.

YOUR FLESH WILL NOT WANT TO FORGET

Have you ever been hurt by someone like these Jews were hurt by the Samaritans? You ask, *"When will it quit hurting?"* Probably, when you get to Heaven, but as long as you live down here the devil will test your love walk. We can take comfort in the fact, God has a book of remembrance, and He knows all things. (See: Mal 3:16)

Carnal Christians often let their flesh dominate them. That's why we need to let the love of God constrain us, so we can grow out of the babyhood stage of carnality and become mature believers, walking by the light of the Word; in light of *the law of love*.

Friend, you have to let the love of God in you set you free in Jesus' Name. God's love shed abroad in our hearts will eventually lead us to victory in life, because God's love never fails. The God-kind of love is always victorious.

TIME FOR A HEART CHECK-UP
by Steve Young

As we grow older in life, we are encouraged to have an annual physical check-up which includes a heart examination with a cardiologist. In doing so, the doctor checks for blood pressure, pulse rate, stress tests, circulation, hardening of arteries, and for any abnormalities.

Likewise throughout all our life, we should have a reoccurring examination with our Master Physician – our Heavenly Father, for a heart check-up. When He examines your heart, will He find areas of sin, hardened attitudes, bitterness, or unforgiveness, that needs repaired and intervention?

Notice I mentioned unforgiveness. Unforgiveness is now classified in the medical books as a disease. Per Dr. Steven Standiford, chief of surgery at the Cancer Treatment Centers of America, *"refusing to forgive makes people sick and keeps them that way."* "It's important to treat emotional wounds or disorders because they really can hinder someone's reactions to the treatments, even someone's willingness to pursue treatment," Standiford explained.

Of all cancer patients, 61 percent have forgiveness issues, and of those, more than half are severe, according to the research by Dr. Michael Barry, a Pastor and the Author of the book, **The Forgiveness Project**. *"Harboring these negative emotions, this anger and hatred, creates a state of chronic anxiety,"* he said.

Likewise it's even more important to seek The Lord for His treatment of our forgiveness of sin, and our forgiveness toward others. The Psalmist wrote, "Create in me a clean heart, O God, and renew a right a right spirit within me." (Psalm 51:10 NKJV) Having a *"clean heart"* consists of being uncontaminated and free from sin. One such sin is unforgiveness, as Jesus Himself said, **"For if you forgive those who sin against you, your heavenly Father will forgive you. But, if you refuse to forgive others, your Father will not forgive your sins."** (Matthew 6: 14-15 NLT) Note that it requires us to take action – forgive others.

Jesus also said, *"Blessed are the pure in heart, for they shall see God."* (Matthew 5:8) The Greek word for "pure" heart is, *katharos* (kath-ar-oss): one without blemish, clean, undefiled, and pure. One of the ways to have a cleansed / pure heart, is to forgive others just as God forgives you. God is no respecter of persons (Acts 10:34), and neither should we.

I DON'T DO GRUMPY
by Barbara J. White

I recently had the pleasure of meeting the sweetest lady. Her countenance shone with the joy of the Lord. Although in her mid-seventies, she was filled with hope and plans for her future. Five years ago she became a widow. You would expect that her vision for her future would have declined. But not at all.

As she shared her vision and call of God on her life, my friend and I listened in amazement. She was filled with a strong *purpose* and *determination* to serve the Lord with gladness and be a blessing to others.

Finally, her words summed up a secret to her life of victory and strong godly desire— "I DON'T DO GRUMPY"!

Wow! Her words said it all—she really meant that she had made a quality decision, not to live a life of discontentment, irritability, being ill-tempered and grouchy.

You know what kind of life this is? It is a life of *living in "the Spirit"* and refusing to allow the flesh, the cares of this world, troubles and trials, to get her down. She had a close relationship with her Lord and Savior, and the Holy Spirit, and she knew it was possible to overcome anything with a joyful attitude flowing out of her spirit.

Let this gracious attitude be your attitude. When things and life get difficult and you are tempted to get grumpy, stop and allow the Holy Spirit and the Word of God to rise up in you and say NO DEVIL, not today!

This is called *the good fight of faith*—we must be a doer of the Word and let the life of Jesus rise to the ascendency and prevail over all the negative feelings and soulish, fleshly desires. This includes ignoring what you see and feel. You can do it in the power of the Holy Spirit and overcome every time. Never give up. Victory belongs to you all the time!

THE HARVEST IS RIPE
BATTLE STATIONS, BATTLE CALL
by Marcella Burnes

The harvest is ripe
It's all around
The harvest its ripe
It's falling on the ground

The GOD of the MOUNTAIN III

Bride of Christ, you are called
The wedding is happening as the fruit begins to fall.
Trinidad and Tobago — these are places we should go
Paraguay, poorest of all
A country being redeemed from the fall.
Peering these and customs please
Places we should be about on our knees
People reconciled with The Lord
Coming to Jesus in massive hordes
Cries of help me, send relief
Mercenaries of belief
Faltering not at the call
PREACH
The Gospel to one and ALL

Fifty percent should be the Sent
Fifty percent should do the send

In record numbers I will send
Be prepared for the win
BATTLE STATION
BATTLE CALL
JESUS LOVES ONE AND ALL

How lovely on the mountain are the feet of them who bring GOOD NEWS!!! – Isaiah 52:7

THE DEAD CAME BACK TO LIFE
by Jim Andrews

Matthew 10:7-8 KJV
7 And as ye go, preach, saying, The kingdom of heaven is at hand.
8 Heal the sick, cleanse the lepers, raise the dead, cast out devils: freely ye have received, freely give.

I received an urgent phone call from a neighbor, he said something was wrong with him; he was physically sick. He had taken meds and now he wasn't breathing right. He said, *"Help!"* I immediately went to his house, I arrived and he called out for me. He couldn't see, his vision had been effected. I took his pulse and it was faint. He collapsed in my arms with no pulse. I commanded death to leave and cursed the effects of the meds. He immediately started breathing—he had came back to life! WHAT A MIGHTY GOD WE SERVE! The dead came back to life.

His life was changed that day. He asked what language I was praying in. I said I was praying in the Spirit, the evidence of speaking in tongues spoken of in Acts 2:4 in the Christian Bible.

He said he wanted to be filled with the Spirit. I prayed for him and he received. His life was never the same. God had given him his life back and he had a closer relationship with God. He was gloriously filled with the Holy Spirit and later stated that for three days he could only speak in his new language.

> Mark 16:17-18 KJV
> 17 And these signs shall follow them that believe; In my name shall they cast out devils; they shall speak with new tongues;
> 18 They shall take up serpents; and if they drink any deadly thing, it shall not hurt them; they shall lay hands on the sick, and they shall recover.

GOD'S AWESOME PLAN
by Karen Y. Ranney
The following exerpt was taken from
"God's Plan One New Man"
▪ Used by Permission.

What an exciting time to be living in! What a privilege to be part of God's awesome plan! This is one of the most exciting times of human history! The Bride is being made ready for her Bridegroom, Yeshua, (Jesus) the Messiah! The Church, the Body, is being restored to its covenant roots. Wow! As Gentiles, we are blessed to be part of it. O God's wonderful grace and mercy! We are privileged to be grafted into the Root, Yeshua, our Messiah, becoming one with the Jewish Messianic believers and thereby receiving the covenant blessings along with them. We see this in Ephesians 3:3-6.

God is restoring the Body of Christ to its Messianic and Hebrew roots. This is so precious, and we get to be part of it. As the Body of Christ, we have lost the understanding of our inheritance in Christ and the Hebrew roots. That is why it is so exciting to see the Messianic movement bringing Jew and Gentile into oneness. "Having abolished in his flesh the enmity, even the law of commandments contained in ordinances; for to make in Himself of twain <u>One New Man</u>, so making peace" (Ephesians 2:15 KJV). We can learn about our lost inheritance through our precious Jewish Messianic brothers and sisters in the Lord and through those grafted in by the blood of Christ. "So that you, with all God's people, will be given strength to grasp the breadth, length, height and depth of the Messiah's love, 19 yes, to know it, even though it is beyond all knowing, so that you will be filled with all the fullness of God" (Ephesians 3:18-19, CJB)). The whole reason for becoming one with God's chosen people is that we can comprehend His great love and be filled with His fullness. What an incredible picture of Christ and His Church, and we are the recipients. Praise God!

What an awesome privilege we have as Gentiles to learn His amazing plan and ways. We get to be a part of God's chosen people, being grafted in, and being a light and instrument for Him to use to help the Jewish people to see and know God's gracious and great love for them through Yeshua, the

Messiah. It is a very *high calling*! We pray that we may be worthy of the calling that God has put upon us. I pray that we would allow God to mold and make us into His likeness so that we can be prepared to have His love for Him and His love for His chosen people, Israel. Especially, I pray that through understanding His great love for us as Gentiles, we would truly have the love Yeshua has for His chosen people.

PATIENCE
by Lynn Whitlock Jones

"For God is not unjust. He will not forget how hard you have worked for him and how you have shown your love to him by caring for other believers, as you still do. Our great desire is that you will keep on loving others as long as life lasts, in order to make certain that what you hope for will come true. Then you will not become spiritually dull and indifferent. Instead, you will follow the example of those who are going to inherit God's promises because of their faith and endurance. God's promises bring hope. For example, there was God's promise to Abraham. Since there was no one greater to swear by, God took an oath in His own Name, saying: *"I will certainly bless you, and I will multiply your descendants beyond number. Then Abraham waited patiently, and he received what God had promised."* - Hebrews 6:10-15 NLT

Our Western world culture has become impatient, instant gratification people. Most everything is available at our fingertips, either by internet or satellite. Our food is microwave ready in seconds, or drive-thru fast. We expect results, and we expect things to happen in our lives the same way as information or food is delivered.

However, God and His promises are not bound by time or by our expectation of instant gratification. In the Scripture above, God had made promises to Abraham and through faith and patience he inherited those promises. It says that Abraham waited patiently. I have heard it said that patience is a virtue. This means that patience is a moral character quality. It is a quality displayed to others and is a statement of trust.

Abraham trusted that God would not and could not lie. He trusted that God was faithful and that trust produced hope and endurance.

I have had occasions where I have had to trust in, hope on and rely upon God's Word to me. Each time I get impatient, I am reminded that I will receive God's promises if I do not give up and if I will *endure*.

God has given all of us promises; promises in His Word, promises through prophecies, and promises spoken to us by His Holy Spirit. If you haven't seen the promises come to pass with your physical eyes, look with your spiritual eyes. See it in the realm of faith and then watch it happen in the physical realm.

I want to encourage you. Have hope, endurance and patience in the process!

> God is not a man, that He should lie, nor a son of man, that He should repent. Has He said, and will He not do? Or has He spoken, and will He not make it good?
> — Numbers 23:19

GOD COMPLETES HIS PROMISES
by Susan E. Kirk

Matthew 18:19
Again, truly I tell you that if two of you on earth agree about anything they ask for, it will be done for them by my Father in heaven.

The night continued. We arrived at the church. Hallelujah! What was the first thing that I saw? I saw Carmen, my friend who lives across the street from the church, kneeling on the ground, looking to heaven, praying. I was overwhelmed with many emotions but mostly gratitude. But Carmen got up and ran down the street. I was confused.

We went into the church. The Pastors were happy to see us. Cesar and John apologized. I asked about Carmen. As the explanation unfolded, I just wept with gratitude.

You see, they thought that we were kidnapped or dead or

both. When we did not arrive with John and Cesar, the entire church began praying for our safety and arrival. Carmen was going to the homes of the church members to announce our safe arrival. Some of the ladies came to the church to celebrate answered prayers. That night, I realized that God had blessed me with a strong, spiritual, believing family. God continues to bless me with His children.

When you go before the throne of God, go believing, go in faith, go with good intentions. The key is to go. God is there. He is waiting for you to ask. He is waiting for you to believe. He is waiting for you to know that He completes His promises. What really happened that night? God walked me through believing in Him. He manifested miracles in police officers and a Catholic couple. He gave me the power to believe when circumstances were screaming otherwise.

Again, focus on God's promises. God completes His promises. God answered all our prayers that night. Unannounced to me, many of God's children (prayer warriors) were praying for me that night. We were not alone. We were in great company…God and His prayer warriors. I still thank God for all who pray for me because I know the power in prayer and God's promises.

Again, God showed me the reality of His promises that dark and rainy night in Mexico. Where and when has He shown you the reality of His promises? Who are your prayer warriors? Remember them, all of them, and give God thanks daily for His promises and prayer warriors.

THE LOVE OF MONEY
by Michael Nokes

As a young boy I often daydreamed, you know the kind of dreams where you have tons of money and never have another unmet need. So as I grew into a young man I slowly developed into the belief and strategy of what I called, "Layered Savings". I discovered that I was good at saving money and investing. Yet I never felt satisfied. Upon my first milestone, I confided in a close friend and immediately suffered envies effects. So, I decided to hide my savings and never ever spoke of them. In fact I lived as if I had none, literally. I was generally a good young man but I was moving fast toward being like the young rich man that asked Jesus a question in Matthew 19:16-24 (KJV). With that frame of mind, I would have never guessed that my story would take such a dramatic turn.

At the time of my testimony of transformation (change), you know the one where I found Him for REAL! Okay let me get REAL, He found me, which felt like me finding Him! Money and things were everything to me. They gave me my security. They gave me the only peace I knew. But it was all an *illusion*, created by a series of *lies* that Satan had introduced and I had accepted. My mind was his sponge and I fought to see (think) clearly. But I could not. And then God's light shined on the illusion. My mind was freed. I was free. My heart began to see a whole new world around me, one filled with amazement. Where the foolish things were the only things that mattered!

> I Timothy 6:10 KJV
> "For the love of money is the root of all evil: which while some coveted after, they have erred from the faith, and pierced themselves through with many sorrows."

> I Corinthians 1:27 KJV
> "But God hath chosen the foolish things of the world to confound the wise; and God hath chosen the weak things of the world to confound the things which are mighty;"

Maybe I should stop here, but I won't. I will drop a few more thoughts to digest. Jesus came to set the captives free. *The love of money* is bondage or captivity. God NEEDS us to TRUST Him, in which it is impossible unless you devote DILIGENTLY the time to learn of Him. How do you self-assess? When you think of money, what thoughts and feelings are associated with it? Do you truly understand that God can supply all your needs according to His riches in glory? Deeper, do you understand that He wants to? And even deeper, do you understand that you have a NEED to NEED HIM in exactly that way?

Thank God he sent His Son Jesus to shine His light, dispel the darkness, and *set the captives free* of which I was one! And all I did was humbly SEEK Him every day.

ON THE ROAD AGAIN
by Ron Kelley

As an electrician and traveling wherever the work was available, I was working for another contractor, although I had the same license myself (a ticket of value).

I was asked to pick up a Company Truck near the Verdigris River and then go to Seminole (in the opposite direction) to do a little repair job; it will only take a couple of hours—I was told. But on site the switchgear was massive with heavy back plates which had to be removed to get access to the repair.

This 2 hour repair was NOT simple and took many more hours getting behind large cables of high voltage and into several large switch gear cabinets.

But that was only a small portion of this day's travels. After finishing, I still had to go to a small city in the northern Texas to meet the rest of the team and be ready to go onto a job site out in the middle of nowhere in the Oklahoma panhandle. The job was hidden from view and very hard to find, and I had to be there before 6:00am the next morning.

The story I wish to relate is: *God watches over His people*, making sure they arrive safely. This is what happened on the way. Finishing the Seminole project, I'd skipped lunch, so out on the highway I stopped at a truck stop near the Oklahoma, Texas line. I decided it was time to get supper, [almost 10:00pm] and a hot meal and lots of coffee for the road; also, a large iced drink to keep me awake.

The isolated two-lane highway was a straight line for miles; no wonder drivers go to sleep. That's exactly what I did. Traveling at cruising speed (70 mph) I had a full stomach, hot coffee, a warm cab and my eyes closed. My hands were three to four inches lower than the horn on the steering wheel. I was comfortable and all alone.

Suddenly, I realized someone was honking the horn. I heard the noise, "Hooooaaaaannnkkk!" "Hooooaaaaannnkkk!" "Hooooaaannnkkk!!!" and a voice shouted: *"WAKE-UP!"* I was angling out of my lane and heading straight for a farmer's silo and a bunch of metal buildings. I came to just in time to get back on the road. The Lord had to have blaired on the horn, my hands were no where near the horn button and there was no other vehicles on the road with me. It was 2-3 am when I arrived at the motel in Texas. Praise the Lord, I was priviledged to continue and not destroy my employer's vehicle.

The Lord has guarded me like this many times. He has *told* me to go another way, because an accident was on my planned route or if a storm was crossing up ahead the Lord would *tell* me to slow down. Once I asked: Why? His *answer* was there is 100 mph wind ahead and I do not want you there. I *listen* to the Lord while traveling, He is always mindful of me to keep me safe. When leaving the house I ask for His help and protection on the road and He is always there. PRAISE THE LORD!

DISTRACTIONS
by Bruce A. Higgins

TOO MUCH PRESSURE

When the Lord unfolded these steps to knowing His will to me, He stressed how important the final step was. He told me as believers, we put too much pressure on ourselves trying to please Him. All God requires is for us to follow our hearts and live our lives by His Holy Word.

You must realize that there is a devil who hates you, because you are trying to please God. As I stated earlier, the devil pressures the believer from the outside in; he comes to our minds to get us off track.

WATCH OUT FOR DISTRACTIONS

The enemy uses distractions, even good money-making distractions, to steal our time away from serving God. Even the devil can't stop you outright from serving God. He will try to get you so busy with other stuff, even stuff that is not in its own right sinful. It becomes sinful when you put it before God.

Take owning a speed boat as an example. There is nothing sinful about owning a boat. But, when the same instrument that can be a lot of fun and a family activity starts to come between you and going to church on Sundays; that's when it is sinful. That's where the devil is headed. He wants you so tied up in taking your boat to the lake every weekend that you start missing church.

The boat won't heal you when you are sick. The boat can't provide the peace you need in life, and most of all, it is a poor example to your kids and family members that you are putting the boat ahead of God and church.

But on the flip-side of this, it wouldn't be wrong if there was a special weekend and you missed a Sunday service to have a special family get-together. You see, you can fall in the ditch on either side of the road, can't you?

WORSHIP WORDS
by Roger K. Lane III

When preaching in Hawaii. The Lord asked me to share with His people about words in the Classic Amplified version to worship God with. Each member of the Trinity. God the Father, Son, and Holy Ghost. You know Paul talking about Christ and the Church? After worshipping with these words, they were then to bring any concerns before Him. I've done this for awhile now. All I can say is wow!

The words: I worship, respect, reverence, notice, regard, honor, prefer, venerate, esteem, defer, praise, love, admire exceedingly, conduct myself purely and modestly, appreciate, prize, adore, am devoted to, deeply love, and enjoy You Father, Jesus and Holy Spirit. (Ephesians 5:33; 1 Peter 3:2 AMPC)

THE SEARCH
by William Paul Howard

For years I traveled this road all alone.
Searching yes looking for a place to call home.
I tried this and that, never feeling God where I was at.
People came and people went,
but I was looking for the One Who was sent.
I looked high and I looked low.
I could not find Him on my own.

One Sunday afternoon a Preacher came to our house
I'll never forget the words that came out of his mouth
The service starts at 7, but I'll wait till 8
For you young man I'll start the service late.

So I got ready and off to church I went.
Another hour wouldn't matter after all the time searching I had spent.
In the service that night they spoke in a strange toungue.
When the invitation was given to the alter I did run.
I gave my heart to Jesus, God's only Son

He's the One I had been looking for my journey had just begun.

If you are also searching for that inner peace
Let me point you to in the right direction
Your destiny you've finally reached.
Oh the joy you will find and you'll have peace of mind.
Let me introduce you to Jesus, my Saviour and my Brother.
He will always be with you, He will be closer than no other.

∽

LIFE AND DEATH; DEATH AND LIFE BIRTHING PAINS
by Marcella Burnes

Were born among pain, tears, rejoicing and cheers
We die among tears, pain, and unknown fears .
BUT WHAT IF……… we have it backwards.
WHAT IF……. we should sorrow at a birth.
WHAT IF…….shouts of rejoicing and backslapping,
And Hallelujahs when we leave this earth!
WHAT IF ……

God's Waiting Room.
Just as the family said good-bye
and the lady slipped to the other side,
Amidst all the family's grief, pain and tears,
I hear a growing roar and resounding cheers.
In God's waiting room on the other side
Rejoicing, laughing and hearty welcomes do abide.

Another one has appeared
Graduated and come up here.
Father hath prepared a place for thee,
We are so happy, hurry, run, let's go see.
Mourning in the physical worldly scene
Glorious morning in the heavenly's beam!

Slipping away seems so hard,
Passing from this dirt and Earth's yard!
But the Word of God has said
Your better off the day you are dead.
Ecclesiastes 7:1
Father, it's over their race here is run!
However on the other side
This Heavenly Eternal Life
In God's Waiting Room abide

WHY WE SHOULD FOCUS ON THE BEAM
by Michael Nokes

"Dedicated to Heather, Jacob, Michael Noah, Zane, Grayson, and My Baby in Heaven"

Matthew 7:5 KJV
"Thou hypocrite, FIRST CAST OUT THE BEAM OUT OF THINE OWN EYE; and then shalt thou see clearly to cast out the mote out of thy brother's eye."

Here is a couple of COMMANDS from our Heavenly Father that call us to introspection:

I Peter 1:15-17 (KJV) says, "But as he which hath called you is holy, so BE YE HOLY IN ALL MANNER OF CONVERSATION; Because it is written, BE YE HOLY; for I am holy. And if ye call on the Father, who without respect of persons judgeth according to every man's work, PASS THE TIME OF YOUR SOJOURNING HERE IN FEAR:

I John 3:3 (KJV) says, "And every man that hath this hope in him PURIFIETH HIMSELF, even as he is pure."

There are several reasons why our Heavenly Father directs His children to prioritize the inward process of purification. Remember He loves His other children too, so he wants us to see clearly before we try to help our brethren. However, the mere thoughts associated with fulfilling the commands of God can be overwhelming if we do not understand His ways and rewards. It's more comfortable to ignore our own brokenness and instead focus our energy on helping others. We use the tactic of avoidance. And I am sure we can all guess whose bright idea avoidance is, especially when it gets whispered in our ear coupled with fear of the unknown.

When we ignore doing the work that God's Word has directed us to, it is more than disobedience to our Father; it's self-defeating. We can even delve into self-exaltation and pride in order to hide avoidance. Think about all the precious time we are wasting. What do we think God will do with the unprofitable servant? (Read: Matthew 25:14-30) Remember that God WILL resist the proud, but He WILL EMBRACE the humble.

2 Timothy 2:20-21 KJV
"But in a great house there are not only vessels of gold and of silver, but also of wood and of earth; and some to honour, and some to dishonour. If a man therefore PURGE HIMSELF from these, he shall be a vessel unto honour, sanctified, and meet for the master's use, and prepared unto every good work.

When we focus on ourselves, it takes our excuses away. It causes us to grow and mature in our faith. Keeping our focus off judgment and on inward reflection keeps us in humility. We do this because we love and trust God and because we have the wisdom to *fear* Him. It makes it easier to forgive and frees us from the bondage of the enemy. Love and Wisdom applied with Humility serves to draw mankind to the Lord. It allows goodness and mercy to rule and reign in our heart over anger and bitterness. It sets us free from—the bondage of SELF!

GOD IS STILL SPEAKING TO MEN
by Aaron Jones

The organization I was once with, asked me to leave because: 'they said' God no longer talks to men, and that everything He was ever going to say is in the King James [version] Bible. ...Really???

Yet, I have spent the last 25+ years walking by what I hear

HIM SAY. I trust that VOICE with my future, my family's future, our finances, business decisions, etc… I've banked everything on it. HE HAS NEVER FAILED ME, NOT ONCE!

Have I missed it? Yes, over and over, but He is teaching me, training me to hear better, tuning my spiritual ear to His frequency. So that more and more I'm walking in harmony with *His plan* for my life. It's an everyday adventure and I am excited about the future!

With the many accounts (in both Old and New Testament) of GOD SPEAKING TO MEN; it is sad that men miss this vital blessing for their lives.

> Genesis 31:11
> And THE ANGEL OF GOD SPAKE unto me in a dream, saying, Jacob: And I said, Here am I.
>
> Genesis 8:15
> Then GOD SPOKE to Noah, saying,
>
> Exodus 6:2
> And GOD SPOKE to Moses and said to him: "I am the LORD.
>
> Job 33:15-16
> 15 In a dream, in a vision of the night, when deep sleep falleth upon men, in slumberings upon the bed; 16 Then He openeth the ears of men, and sealeth their instruction,

Matthew 3:17 KJV
And lo a VOICE FROM HEAVEN, SAYING, This is my beloved Son, in whom I am well pleased.

John 10:27 KJV
My sheep hear MY VOICE, and I know them, and they follow me:

Acts 9:4, 7 KJV
4 Then he fell to the ground, and heard a VOICE SAYING to him, "Saul, Saul, why are you persecuting Me?"
7 And the men who journeyed with him stood speechless, hearing a VOICE but seeing no man.

Act 9:10-11 NKJV
10 Now there was a certain disciple at Damascus named Ananias; and to him THE LORD SAID in a vision, "Ananias." And he said, "Here I am, Lord."

Acts 11:7
And I heard a VOICE SAYING unto me, Arise, Peter; slay and eat.

Romans 8:14
For as many as are LED BY THE SPIRIT OF GOD, they are the sons of God.

Revelations 1:10, 12
10 I was in the Spirit on the Lord's day, and heard

behind me a GREAT VOICE, as of a trumpet, ...

12 And I turned to see THE VOICE THAT SPAKE with me. And being turned, I saw seven golden candlesticks;

Revelation 3:20
Behold, I stand at the door, and knock: If any man HEAR MY VOICE, and open the door, I will come in to him, and will sup with him, and he with me.

Listen, listen, listen closely—GOD IS STILL SPEAKING to men. I deal with many natural earthly Authors every day, interesting is the fact—they can all still talk. How much more can the supernatural Author of the world's best-selling Book, The Bible still speak to us; if we will only listen.

He that hath an ear to hear, let him hear—WHAT THE SPIRIT OF GOD IS SAYING!

HEAVEN KNOWS DAD
by Marty Clancy

I had the privilege of preaching the message at my Dad's funeral. The Lord had given me the message, **"Heaven knows Dad. Does Heaven know you?"** I want to share what the Lord gave me:

- Hebrews 12:23 NKJV says we are "registered in Heaven". On Earth we register for all kinds of things like bridal registries, baby showers, etc. The registry in Heaven is forever!

- Philippians 3:20 says our "citizenship is in Heaven". Being a citizen of the USA is great but being born again to heavenly citizenship is the most important one!

- In I Peter 1:4 we see that God has given us an "inheritance incorruptible and undefiled that does not fade away, reserved in Heaven for you." More good news! We may get an inheritance on Earth, but the inheritance waiting for us in Heaven is incomparable!

If we've done our registration, made our reservation, and checked our citizenship, then we are ready to receive our inheritance from the Father. When we accept Jesus as our Savior we are born again into the heavenly family. We have the Holy Spirit as proof of our new birth, deposited in us at salvation. As the song goes, "There's a new name written down in Glory" and we are registered in the Lamb's Book of Life (Rev. 21:27).

II Timothy 2:19 says the Lord knows those who are His. Rejoice because like Heaven knows my Dad, Heaven knows you, and glorious, incorruptible treasures are in store for you, prepared by our Heavenly Father!

WALKING BY FAITH
by Rachel V. Jeffries

When we do not see evidence of things we hope for, what do we do? So often our minds wonder what is going to happen. Did you know you can have thoughts of doubt in your head, but your heart is full of faith? When someone has passed from this life before us, especially if it is your mate, you wonder how life can continue. Well, for sure it won't be the same, it will be different. God's desire for you and me is to have a good life no matter what the circumstances are. I have shared with you many times how I came up against impossible situations that made life seem impossible.

THE FAITH TEST

I have lived long enough now to tell you; my faith was tested. One thing I did not allow myself to do and that is to speak against God in any way. My heart knew the Lord and how He works. Even though it was hard, my heart knew the Lord would bring me into a new life. My head said, differently but making the decision to go by faith was easier than crashing in negative emotions and saying things I did not want to happen.

IS IT CRAZY OR GOOD SENSE?

Walking by faith may seem crazy to some but it is so much better for us physically, mentally and spiritually. We can climb out of any hole, or we can walk by faith and not go into the hole but stay above it all. Either way, God is there to help us get to the other side.

I speak peace to you today in spirit, soul and body. Be blessed immensely!

Prayer: Lord, I thank you for all you are to me. You have blessed me so many times. When it has seemed, there was no way out of difficulty you have brought me forward in life and promoted me. I love you Lord. Help me to see that you're making new paths for my life. In Jesus Name! AMEN!

Confession: Confession brings possession. Lord, I confess your wholeness in my soul, (mind, will and emotions). I speak to the mountains and say, *"Be removed and cast into the sea."* No matter how I feel, I walk by faith and not by sight. I doubt not in my head but have faith in my heart. When my head says, *"It cannot be,"* my heart says, *"It shall be."* GLORY!

>2 Corinthians 5:7
>I walk by faith even when I cannot see.

>Romans 10:17
>Faith comes by hearing, and hearing by the Word of God.

TRUST IN THE PROCESS
by Lynn Whitlock Jones

One of my favorite sweet treats to make is a mini peanut butter cookie with a Reese's cup in the middle. They are not hard to make if you follow the directions.

For the holidays I always make these treats as well as several others to give to our customers, friends and family. As I was making the cookies before Christmas, and I made a batch that browned just a little too much. Of course, my husband and family ate them anyway because they love me. And I made a new batch to give away.

The directions said to cook 8 minutes. Looking at the tops of the cookies in their little muffin tin nests, they just did not look done to me. So I added a couple of more minutes to the timer and cooked them too long. I did not trust that the directions given were right and I decided to change them myself. My decision cost me time and money.

Philippians 1:6 says, "Being confident of this very thing, that He who has begun a good work in you will complete it until the day of Jesus Christ;" When we place our confidence in Him and trust that the good work He has started He will also complete, then we turn out just right.

The Word of God is full of directions given to us by the

Father through men of God, who were inspired by the Holy Spirit to write them down for us to read and follow. When we decide to change the directions to suit our thoughts and desires, we mess things up. Those decisions cost us dearly.

So Holy Spirit reminded me through a batch of too dark cookies that we should trust in the directions given and not change them to suit us.

DO YOU FEEL HIM NOW?
by William Paul Howard

Won't keep my Words to myself
I take my Bible down, Won't put it back on the shelf
It might be you, who is in need,
I am speaking from the heart now.

O Oh yea-oh, I'm a Christian cause I want to be
Jesus came down here, for you and me
He's not over yet, you can feel Him now
O Oh Yeah, I'm a Christian cause I want to be
You can feel Him like it's 1993---O Oh Yeah
Do you feel Him now?

Got another Word now
Speaking truth to a congregation
I will not be stopped, NO Not Now

The GOD of the MOUNTAIN III

I am speaking from the heart now.

O Oh yea-oh, I'm a Christian cause I want to be
Jesus came down here for you and me
He's not over yet, You can Feel Him Now
O Oh yeah, I'm a Christian cause I want to be
You can feel him like it's 1993---O oh Yeah
Do you Feel Him Now?

You can get saved If you want to
(O Oh yea-oh, I'm a Christian cause I want to be)
You can go to Heaven
Good-bye to that Old way of life
Stop freaking and just let it be
Don't have to wait till there's no one around
(O Oh yea-oh, I'm a Christian cause I want to be)
It's time to give into your inter-being
You know it's time
Come go with me

He is coming!
He is coming!
He is coming!
He is coming!
He is Coming!
He is coming Back!
O Oh yea-oh, I'm a Christian cause I want to be
His love is an Abyss for your heart not to miss, yeah
Do you feel Him Now?

O Oh yeah I'm a Christian cause I want to be
Jesus came down here for you and me
He's not over yet, you can feel him now.
O Oh yeah, I'm a Christian cause I want to be
You can feel Him like it's 1993---) O Oh yeah
Do you feel him now?
I know you feel Him Now!

STAY IN THE MIDDLE OF THE ROAD
by Bruce A. Higgins

I was living in Tulsa, Oklahoma, next to a very nice man. He and his wife divorced and he finally got custody of his children. The girl was about fourteen years of age, and one day I witnessed to her about accepting Christ into her life.

She was a very sweet kid and after a awhile I told her family about this church in town, that had a great youth program. Well, someone at school took her to the youth outreach and she, her brother and her dad got saved and involved in the church.

One day after she had gone to this church close to a year, she saw me coming home. She started in with a Scripture out of Hebrews: *"Not forsaking the assembling of ourselves together, as the manner of some is; and exhorting one another: and so much teh more, as ye see the day approach-*

ing." (He 10:25) Then she started in (a girl who just got saved less than a year earlier, speaking to me, who at the time had been in full-time ministry for 25 years) telling me that I was in sin because I wasn't in church every Sunday morning. [There is such a thing as respecting your elders.]

I told her, as I had told her father several times before, that I travel a great deal and sometimes getting home very late on Staurday night, my wife and I would not make Sunday morning service, but would go Sunday nights and Wednesday nights when there was more teaching out of God's Word, which I preferred.

That wasn't good eough for her, even when I told her I speak Sunday mornings all over the country, but when I am home we go to other services. It didn't matter to her that we were going twice a week and many times three times, when she only went once a week. I finally told her it was none of her business, when i saw I was dealing with a *religious spirit* out of Hell.

I later, thought to myself, *"Boy, I liked that girl a whole lot more before she got in church. What happened to her? What happened to that sweet nice kid?"* She got too far in the ditch, it was a: her way or the highway mentality.

My Brothers and Sisters, don't go to the left or oight of the road, but stay right in the middle of it.

WATCH YOUR WALK
by Brian Ohse

Do you know who has been impacted by your walk?

Do you know who you've driven away?

Who has been changed because of Him (in you)?

Who has longed to know this Christ you serve?

Have you lost your focus?

It's not about you, but He Who dwells in you. Make no mistake people, time is short before Jesus returns. The signs are all around us: Do you see them? If not, ask the Holy Spirit to reveal them to you. Even as He gave me deeper understanding early this morning, pertaining to four words.

So receive and understand that: He was broken in spirit that ours might be made whole. He was bruised for our iniquities, that we might be healed. He was beaten for our transgressions, that we would no longer live defeated lives. He spilled His blood, that we might receive His love. For without the shedding of blood, there is no remission, or payment for sin.

So don't close up when you are hurting; instead, let your pain be healing for others. Show *compassion*, just like Jesus did in Matthew 5. Let's look at this and see what the Spirit reveals, starting with verse 1, "And seeing the multitudes..." Does pain rise up in you when you see how lost so many people are? Do you cry out in your spirit for them? Then "When he was set." Only when you are in position will people come to you. So recognize preparation time is very important.

Now verse 2: "He opened his mouth and taught them." When you open your mouth, it must be filled with teaching grace, not condemnation or hardness of heart. For you must see them as He does.

Let's continue with verse 3: "Blessed are the poor in spirit." Why are people weak in spirit? They never had proper teaching, yet they were hungry for truth. I'm reminded of the verse found in Galatians 6:1, "Ye which are spiritual, restore such a one in the spirit of meekness." In other words, you that have been *given revelation* and *knowledge* by the Holy Spirit, don't be arrogant or haughty about what you know—walk in *humility*.

Now verse 4: "Blessed are they that mourn." Strongs' said: You feel pain inside for them, your touched with the feelings of their "infirmities," meaning their physical or mental weakness. So let brokeness do a work inside you.

DILIGENTLY STUDY
SHOW GOD YOUR HEART
by Aaron Jones

2 Timothy 2:15 KJV
Study to shew thyself approved unto God, a workman that needeth not to be ashamed, rightly dividing the word of truth.

But in several other versions it's translated as:

- New Living Testament (NLT) -- Work hard so you can present yourself to God and receive his approval....

- The NIV, ESV and RSV all say, -- Do your best to present yourself to God as one approved...

- New English Translation (NET) -- Make every effort to present yourself before God as a proven worker ...

> Hebrews 4:12-13 KJV
> 12 For the word of God [is] quick, and powerful, and sharper than any twoedged sword, piercing even to the dividing asunder of soul and spirit, and of the joints and marrow, and [is] a discerner of the thoughts and intents of the heart.
> 13 Neither is there any creature that is not manifest

in his sight: but all things [are] naked and opened unto the eyes of him with whom we have to do.

Most Christians would say the reason they read their Bible is to get a picture of (or to know) God. But is it possible, when we take the time to study God's Word, He takes a look into us? That opening The Book not only reveals God's faithfulness on every page, but that it also reveals to Him our level of faithfulness in every moment we spend studying?

It's a relationship. It's time we (God and I) spend together so that relationship grows. Herein is my approval---when I search for Him, when I sacrifice my schedule, my plans and my time to sit before Him and READ MY BIBLE. It shows THE LOVER of my soul that I want to know Him. My actions (taking time to read and study) shows God my heart..

Some say. *"I just don't have time to read the Bible."*

King Solomon said, "[It is] the glory of God to conceal a thing: but the honour of kings [is] to search out a matter." (Pr 25:2) I am sure that as a king over a nation his schedule was much more filled and hectic than ours!

It's not that you don't have time to read the Bible---it's a heart issue, YOU REALLY DON'T CARE TO READ THE BIBLE. And there too, you are (by your actions) showing God what is in you.

The GOD of the MOUNTAIN III

> 2 Peter 1:19 KJV
> We have also a more sure word of prophecy; whereunto ye do well that ye take heed, as unto a light that shineth in a dark place, until the day dawn, and the day star arise in your hearts:

YOU DON'T HAVE TIME TO 'NOT' READ THE BIBLE! With all of its crime, disease, poverty and war this world is played out and has no more cards to put on the table. The end-game is upon us, Satan has raised the ante; this Earth has nothing left to offer.

Jesus is coming! And He will bring judgement for those who have ignored and rejected Him, and rewards for those who accepted Him and diligently searched for Him (they followed on in His Word to truly know Him).

Your eternal destiny depends on—YOU KNOWING GOD.

> Hebrews 11:6 KJV *(caps added)*
> But without faith [it is] impossible to please [him]: for he that cometh to God must believe that he is, and [that] HE IS A REWARDER OF THEM THAT DILIGENTLY SEEK HIM.

THE WEAPONS OF OUR WARFARE

are not of the flesh, but they are mighty through God to the destruction of human reasonings and strongholds of our enemies.
(2 Corinthians 10:4 pp.)

AUTHORITY OVER SATAN

Isaiah 54:17
Matthew 7:29, 28:18, 10:7, 18:18
Luke 9:1, 10:19
John 12:31, 14:12, 30, 17:15
Romans 6:14, 8:37
1 Corinthians 15:57
2 Corinthians 10:4-5
Ephesians 1:3, 19-21, 4:27, 6:10-17
Colossians 2:10, 15
2 Timothy 1:7
Hebrews 10:13
1 Peter 5:8
1 John 4:4, 7
Revelations 12:11, 21:7

FAITH

Proverbs 3:5
Matthew 17:20, 21:22
Mark 9:23, 11:22-24
Luke 17:5-10
Romans 10:17

1 Corinthians 2:5
2 Corinthians 5:7
Galatians 2:20
Ephesians 2:8, 6:16
Hebrews 11:1, 6
2 Timothy 4:7
James 2:14-26
1 Peter 5:9
1 John 5:4

FORGIVENESS

Exodus 15:26
1 Kings 8:34
Psalm 25:18, 86:5
Jeremiah 31:34
Matthew 6:12-15, 9:6, 18:21-22, 24-35
Mark 2:10, 25-26
Luke 5:21, 24, 6:37, 11:4, 17:3-4, 23:34
Acts 5:31, 13:38, 26:18
2 Corinthians 2:10
Ephesians 1:7
Colossians 2:14
1 John 1:9

HEALING

Exodus 15:26
Psalm 91:3, 6-10, 103:3, 107:20
Proverbs 4:20-22, 17:22
Isaiah 53:5
Jeremiah 30:17

Malachi 4:2
Matthew 4:23, 8:7, 17
Mark 16:18
Luke 1:37, 9:6
John 14:14
Acts 5:16, 10:38
Romans 8:2
Galatians 3:13
Hebrews 2:14
James 5:14-16
1 Peter 2:24
3 John 2

PEACE

Leviticus 26:6
Job 5:24, 22:21
Psalm 4:8, 29:11, 34:14, 37:11, 37, 46:10, 119:165, 122:7
Isaiah 9:7, 26:3, 12, 45:7, 52:7, 53:5
Jeremiah 29:11, 33:6
Matthew 10:13, 34
Luke 1:79, 2:14
John 14:27, 16:33, 20:21
Acts 10:36
Romans 5:1, 8:6, 14:17, 19, 15:33
1 Corinthians 7:15, 14:33
Galatians 5:22
Ephesians 2:14-17
Philippians 4:7, 9
Colossians 1:20, 3:15

2 Thessalonians 3:16
Hebrews 12:14

PROSPERITY

Genesis 2:11-12, 13:2, 24:35, 39:2-6
Deuteronomy 8:18, 16:17, 28:1-13
1 Kings 2:3
2 Chronicles 1:15
Psalm 1:1-3, 37:4, 105:37
Proverbs 3:9-10, 10:22, 13:22, 16:3, 21:20, 22:9, 28:27
Jeremiah 17:7-8
Malachi 3:8-10
Matthew 6:33
Luke 6:38, 16:10-11, 21:1-4
2 Corinthians 8:9, 9:6-8
Galatians 3:14, 3:29, 6:9
Philippians 4:19
3 John 2

PROTECTION

Exodus 14:14
Deuteronomy 31:6
2 Samuel 22:3-4
Job 5:19-27
Psalm 4:8, 5:11, 12:5, 20:1, 23:4, 34:19, 46:1, 57:1, 59:1, 91:1-16, 121:1-8, 138:7, 140:4
Proverbs 2:11
Isaiah 41:10-14, 54:17
Nahum 1:7

Matthew 6:13
Luke 1:68-75
Romans 8:31
2 Thessalonians 3:2-3
2 Timothy 4:18

SALVATION

Mark 8:35
Luke 1:68-75
John 1:12, 29, 3:3, 16, 36
Acts 2:21, 3:19, 4:12, 10:43, 16:30-31
Romans 3:23-24, 5:6, 6:23, 10:9-10
2 Corinthians 5:17
Ephesians 2:8-9
Colossians 1:13-14, 20-22, 2:13-15
1 Peter 2:24
1 John 5:11

CONTRIBUTING AUTHORS' MINISTRY CONTACT INFORMATION
(In Alphabetical Order)

- **Allen, Rachel**
Revolution Revival Ministries
212 West Waco Place
Broken Arrow, OK 74011
(402) 594-6071
revrevmin1@gmail.com

- **Andrews, Jim and Sharon**
Glory In His Presence Ministry, Inc.
Tulsa, OK
(918) 663-5434
andrewszoe0@gmail.com

- **Batty, Jeane**
Jeane Batty Ministries
251 Windridge St.
Branson, MO 65616
(209) 777-7726
jeanebattyministries.com

- **Beattie, Darla Faye**
dmulanax597@yahoo.com
Facebook: Darla Faye

- **Bridges, Ginny**
Virginia Sue Barden Bridges
P.O. Box 3205
Pineville, LA 71361
ginrn1988@hotmail.com

- **Brophy, Renee**
Anointed Ones
c/o Brophy
7828 S Victor Ave., Apt. #6d
Tulsa, OK 74136
eagleatwar@hotmail.com

- **Burnes, Marcella O'Banion**
marcellaburnes@yahoo.com
Contact via the publisher:
ATTN: Marcella Burness
C/O BOLD TRUTH PUBLISHING
606 West 41st Street, 4 Ste.
Sand Springs, OK 74063
boldtruthbooks@yahoo.com

- **Clancy, Marty**
Fresh Proof Ministries, Inc.
P.O. Box 130,
Eagleville, TN 37060
(615) 274-1080
www.freshproof.org
clancyrocks@hotmail.com
Facebook: Fresh Proof Ministries

- **Conley, Steven**
Contact via the publisher:
ATTN: Steven Conely
C/O BOLD TRUTH PUBLISHING
606 West 41st Street, 4 Ste.
Sand Springs, OK 74063
boldtruthbooks@yahoo.com

- **Farmer, Steve**
Pastor Steve Farmer
Open Door Fellowship
405 East Taft
Sapulpa, OK 74066
www.OpenDoorFellowship.com
sfarmer321@cox.net

- **Fern, Rick**
Rick Fern Ministries
P.O. Box 612246
Dallas, TX 75261
http://rickfernministries.com/#/!/giving/
www.rickfernministries. com
Facebook: Rick Fern
Twitter: Rick Fern Ministries @ RFernMinistries
Instagram: Rick Fern Ministries

- **Gottlieb, Adrienne**
Adrienne Gottlieb, J.D.
Santa Fe, NM
www.GodsWisdomForWomen.com
agot@comcast.net
Facebook: God's Wisdom for Women

- **Hicks, Mike**
Minister Michael Hicks
P. O. Box 11491
Oklahoma City, OK 73136
www.YAHJireh.org and Facebook.
Mrhicks58@gmail.com

- **Higgins, Bruce A.**
Bruce Higgins Ministries.
P. O. Box 691427
Tulsa, OK 74169
bahministries@att.net

- **Holloman, Daryl P**
P. O. Box 1649
Broken Arrow, OK 74013-1649 ▪ USA
dphwriter@yahoo.com

- **Howard, William Paul**
Claremore, OK
(918) 521-4661
farmguy@hotmail.com

- **Jeffries, Dr. Rachel V**
Rachel Jeffries International Ministries
P.O. Box 815
Hollister, MO 65673
rachel@rjim.org
Facebook: Rachel Jeffries International Ministries
Facebook: WIDOWS WITH PURPOSE (all caps required)
Website: rjim.org

- **Jones, Aaron**
Aaron Jones Global Net Ministries
Bold Truth Publishing
606 West 41st, Ste. 4
Sand Springs, OK 74063 ▪ USA
(918) 402-4195
www.BoldTruthPublishing.com
boldtruthbooks@yahoo.com
Facebook: Aaron Jones
Pinterest: Bold Truth Publishing

- **Jones, Lynn Whitlock**
His Hands Ministries
(918) 244-3131
www.hishandsministries.org

- **Kelley, Ronald**
Rev. Ron Kelley
Resurrection Ministries
P.O. Box 41
Sand Springs, OK 74063
sparkchaser4eden@gmail.com

- **Kirk, Susan E.**
Thru His Mercy, Inc.,
P.O. Box 5681
McAllen, Texas 78502
(361) 232-9555
www.thruhismercy.org
susankirk@thruhismercy.org

- **Knox, Rhonda**
P.O. Box 450194
Grove, Oklahoma 74345
(918) 964-5095
(918) 786-7535
www.yousaidgoministries.com

- **Lampkin, Bobby**
www.rapkoministries.com
rapkoministries@gmail.com

- **Lane, Roger K. III**
Pastor Roger K. Lane III
Last Say Ministries
P.O. Box 14474
Tulsa, OK 74159
(918) 712-2777

- **Marr, Ed**
Stone Bluff, Haskell, OK
bigedvocal1@gmail.com

- **Moore, Bill**
Pastor Bill Moore
Bikers for Life Inc.
P.O. Box 605
Rhome, Texas 76078
(940) 399-9679
ridingfortheunborn@gmail
Facebook: Bikers for Life
Facebook: Moe-Tv

- **Nokes, Michael**
Michael Nokes Ministries
5103 S Sheridan Rd, #742
Tulsa, OK 74145
(918) 645-7517

- **Ohse, Brian**
Rev. Brian Ohse
Grace Ministries
(913) 416-3426
briandohse59@gmail.com

- **Ranney, Allen and Karen**
Dr. Allen and Dr. Karen Ranney
Jew and Gentile Ministries, Inc.
18463 S. Hickory St.
Sapulpa, OK 74066
(918) 986-4339
www.jewandgentileministries.org
allenranney@yahoo.com
Facebook: jewandgentileministries

- **Ricker, Doug**
Praise and Worship Leader
Last Say Ministries
PO Box 14474
Tulsa, OK 74159
(918) 510-5419
dnjricker@gmail.com

- **Sanders, LisaMarie**
Cleveland, TN
Founder of Well Watered Garden
(*Marriage Restoration & Fasting Group on* Facebook)
L. O. V. E. Ministries
Flowerdeu79@yahoo.com

- **Sanders, Wayne**
Common Ground Ministries
P.O. Box 2811
Broken Arrow, OK 74013
(918) 455-4000
www.cgmok.com
waycom3@gmail.com

- **Steinmetz, William (Bill)**
Bill and Shirley Steinmetz
Casting Cares Ministries, Inc.
(918) 637-6412
Casting-Cares.org
Shirley@casting-cares.org

- **White, Barbara J.**
Faith Ministries International
P.O. Box 79126
Corona, CA 92879
fmint2010@hotmail.com
Facebook: Faith Ministries International
Facebook: Winning Widows

- **Young, Steve**
Doors of Compassion Ministries
P.O. Box 974
Sapulpa, OK 74067-0974
www.doorsofcompassion.org
Facebook: Steve Young
Facebook: Doors of Compassion Ministries

Check out these other Great Books from
BOLD TRUTH PUBLISHING

by Pastor Bill "Moe" Moore
- **5 Months of FAITH**
My Testimony

-----

by Rick Fern
- **ADVENTURES WITH GOD**

See more Books and all of our products at
www.BoldTruthPublishing.com

THE FAVOR OF GOD IS THE ENGINE THAT DRIVES EVERY SUCCESSFUL ENDEAVOR, AND IT IS THE BACKBONE AND THE PROPELLER OF ANY GLORIOUS DESTINY.

Every person on Earth would like to have true peace, hope and joy. Everyone wants to enjoy freedom, glorious victories, success and lasting prosperity. We see and can receive all of these things in the divine favor of God found through a relationship with Jesus Christ.

Available through this ministry and at
AMAZON.COM

Using the ancient Torah teaching cycle (Parashah) as the format, the Author shows/teaches Jesus Christ, Yeshua Messiah, from the first page of the Bible to the last.

"From GOD through Moses to YOU" is an incredible journey through THE TORAH combining revealing word studies, references in both the Hebrew and Greek text, along with prophetic insights and teachings through the Torah, Prophets' and Gospel Portions. Although this is meat from The Word, all the fix'ins are included for several full spiritual meals for anyone hungry for a better understanding of The Bible and a closer walk with Christ.

Available through this ministry and at
AMAZON.COM

Have you ever met an angel? Many have; but according to The Bible, most never know it. The angel(s) appear as normal humans or in another form so that we don't know they are here. God's ANGELS are working among us daily to minister to God's people and carry out their heavenly and sometimes earthly purpose.

This little book is loaded with information that Believers ought and need to know about ANGELS. What do they do? Why are they here? How do they operate in the earth? When do they show up? What does The Bible say about ANGELS?

Available through this ministry and at
AMAZON.COM

www.ingramcontent.com/pod-product-compliance
Lightning Source LLC
Chambersburg PA
CBHW061758110426
42742CB00012BB/1941